EAST OF SUEZ

CEYLON, INDIA, CHINA AND JAPAN

EAST OF SUEZ

CEYLON, INDIA, CHINA AND JAPAN

FREDERIC COURTLAND PENFIELD

GYAN

Published by

GYAN

Gyan Publishing House
5, Ansari Road
Daryaganj, New Delhi-110002
Phone: 011-47034999, 9811692060
E-mail: books@gyanbooks.com

Distribution Network
gyanbooks.com
India, USA, Canada, UK, Australia

ISBN: 978-93-6433-605-5 (HB)

First Published, 1907

2nd Impression 2024

Printed at: Gyan Press, Delhi.

EAST OF SUEZ: CEYLON, INDIA, CHINA AND JAPAN
Author: FREDERIC COURTLAND PENFIELD

EAST OF SUEZ

GULF OF MANAR PEARLING BOAT, AND DIVERS RESTING IN THE WATER

EAST OF SUEZ

CEYLON, INDIA, CHINA AND JAPAN

By

Frederic Courtland Penfield

Author of "Present-Day Egypt," etc.

Illustrated from Drawings and Photographs

"East is East, and West is West, and
never the twain shall meet,
Till Earth and Sky stand presently at
God's great Judgment Seat."
Kipling.

NEW YORK
THE CENTURY CO.
1907

Introductory

IF books of travel were not written the stay-at-home millions would know little of the strange or interesting sights of this beautiful world of ours; and it surely is better to have a vicarious knowledge of what is beyond the vision than dwell in ignorance of the ways and places of men and women included in the universal human family.

The Great East is a fascinating theme to most readers, and every traveler, from Marco Polo to the tourist of the present time, taking the trouble to record what he saw, has placed every fireside reader under distinct obligation.

So thorough was my mental acquaintance with India through years of sympathetic study of Kipling that a leisurely survey of Hind simply confirmed my impressions. Other generous writers had as faithfully taught what China in reality was, and Mortimer Menpes, Basil Hall Chamberlain, and Miss Scidmore had as conscientiously depicted to my understanding the ante-war Japan. Grateful am I, as well, to the legion of tireless writers attracted to the East by recent strife and conquest, who have made Fuji more familiar to average readers than any mountain peak in the United States; who have made the biographies of favorite geishas known even in our hamlets and mining camps, and whose agreeable iteration of scenes on Manila's lunetta compel our Malaysian capital to be known as well as Coney Island and Atlantic City—they have so graphically portrayed and described interesting features that of them nothing remains to be told. But to know Eastern lands and peoples without an intermediary is keenly delightful and compensating.

The travel impulse and longing for first-hand knowledge, native with most mortals, is yearly finding readier expression. Our grandparents earned a renown more than local by crossing the Atlantic to view England and the Continent, while our fathers and mothers exploring distant Russia and the Nile were accorded marked consideration. The wandering habit is as progressive as catching, and what sufficed our ancestors satisfies only in minor degree the longing of the present generation for roving. Hence the grand tour, the circuit of the earth, is becoming an ordinary achievement. And while hundreds of Americans are compassing the earth this year, thousands will place the globe under tribute in seasons not remote.

For many years to come India and Ceylon will practically be what they are to-day, and sluggish China will require much rousing before her national characteristics differ from what they are now; but of Japan it is different, for, having made up their minds to remodel the empire, the sons of Nippon are not doing things by halves, and the old is being supplanted by the new with amazing rapidity.

Introductory

Possibly it is a misfortune to find oneself incapable of preparing a volume of travel without inflicting a sermon upon kindly disposed persons, but a book of journeyings loaded with gentle preachment must at least be a novelty. Travel books imparting no patriotic lesson may well be left to authors and readers of older and self-sufficient nations. A work appealing on common lines to a New World audience would be worse than *banal,* and a conscientious American writer is compelled to describe not alone what he saw, but in clarion notes tell of some things he failed of seeing, for our country, emerging but now from the formative period, and destined to permanently lead the universe in material affairs, is entitled to be better known in the East by its manufactures.

Every piece of money expended in travel is but the concrete form of somebody's toil, or the equivalent of a marketed product: and consequently it is almost unnecessary to remind that industry and thrift must precede expenditure, or to assert that toil and travel bear inseparable relationship. What the American, zigzagging up and down and across that boundless region spoken of as East of Suez, fails to see is the product of Uncle Sam's mills, workshops, mines and farms. From the moment he passes the Suez Canal to his arrival at Hong Kong or Yokohama, the Stars and Stripes are discovered in no harbor nor upon any sea; and maybe he sees the emblem of the great republic not once in the transit of the Pacific. And the products of our marvelous country are met but seldom, if at all, where the American wanders in the East. He is rewarded by finding that the Light of Asia is American petroleum, but that is about the only Western commodity he is sure of encountering in months of travel.

This state of things is grievously wrong, for it should be as easy for us to secure trade in the Orient as for any European nation, and assuredly easier than for Germany. We have had such years of material prosperity and progress as were never known in the history of any people, it is true; but every cycle of prosperity has been succeeded by lean years, and ever will be. When the inevitable over-production and lessened home consumption come, Eastern markets, though supplied at moderate profit, will be invaluable. We are building the Panama Canal, whose corollary *must be* a mercantile fleet of our own upon the seas, distributing the products of our soil and manufactories throughout the world, and Secretary of State Root has made it easy for a better understanding and augmented trade with the republics to the south of us. But America's real opportunity is in Asia, where dwell more than half the people of the earth, for the possibilities of commerce with the rich East exceed those of South America tenfold. Uncle Sam merits a goodly share of the trade of both these divisions of the globe.

The people of the United States must cut loose from the idea that has lost its logic in recent years, that the Pacific Ocean *separates* America from the lands and islands of Asia, and look upon it as a body of water *connecting* us with the bountiful East. The old theory was good enough for our home-building fathers, but is blighting to a generation aspiring to Americanize the globe. The genius of our nation should cause our ploughs and harrows to prepare the valley and delta of the Nile for tillage; be responsible for the whir of more of our agricultural machinery in the fields of India; locate our lathes and planers and drilling machines in Eastern shops, in substitution for those made in England or Germany; be responsible for American locomotives drawing American cars in Manchuria and Korea over rails rolled in Pittsburgh, and induce half the inhabitants of southern Asia to dress in fabrics woven in the United States, millions of the people of Cathay to tread the earth in shoes produced in New England, and all swayed to an appreciation of our flour as a substitute for rice—yes, make it easy to obtain pure canned foods everywhere in China and Japan, even to hear the merry click of the typewriter in Delhi, Bangkok and Pekin.

Do we not already lead in foreign trade? We do, I gratefully admit; but it is because we sell to less favored peoples our grains and fiber in a raw state. Confessedly, these are self-sellers, for not a bushel of wheat or ounce of cotton is sold because of any enterprise on our part—the buyer must have them, and the initiative of the transaction is his.

What economists regard as "trade" in its most advantageous form, is the selling to foreigners of something combining the natural products and the handiwork of a nation—this is the trade that America should look for in the East, and seek it now. It is not wild prophecy that within five years a considerable number of the sovereign people of the country controlling its growth will feel that it is carrying international comity to the point of philanthropy to export cotton to England and Japan to be there fabricated for the wear of every race of Asia, and sold in successful competition with American textiles. In the pending battle for the world's markets Uncle Sam should win trade by every proper means, and not by methods most easily invoked; and let it ever be remembered that shortsightedness is plainly distinct from altruism.

FREDERIC C. PENFIELD.

AUTHORS CLUB, NEW YORK CITY,
January 26, 1907.

CONTENTS

LIST OF ILLUSTRATIONS

List of Illustrations

List of Illustrations

EAST OF SUEZ

EAST OF SUEZ

CHAPTER I

THE WORLD'S TURNSTILE AT SUEZ

WHEN historical novels and "purpose" books dealing with great industries and commodities cease to sell, the vagrant atoms and shadings of history ending with the opening of the two world-important canals might be employed by writers seeking incidents as entrancing as romances and which are capable of being woven into narrative sufficiently interesting to compel a host of readers. The person fortunate enough to blaze the trail in this literary departure will have a superabundance of material at command, if he know where and how to seek it.

The paramount fact-story of all utilitarian works of importance is unquestionably that surrounding the great portal connecting Europe with Asia. As romances are plants of slow growth in lands of the Eastern hemisphere, compared with the New World, the fascinating tale of Suez required two or three thousand years for its development, while that of Panama had its beginning less than four hundred years ago. In both cases the possession of a canal site demanded by commerce brought loss of territory and prestige to the government actually owning it. The Egyptians were shorn of the privilege of governing Egypt through the reckless pledging of credit to raise funds for the completion of the waterway connecting Port Saïd and Suez, and the South American republic of Colombia saw a goodly slice of territory pass forever from her rule, with the Panama site, when the republic on the isthmus came suddenly into being.

Vexatious and humiliating as the incidents must have been to the Egyptians and the Colombians, the world at large, broadly considering the situations, pretends to see no misfortune in the conversion of trifling areas to the control of abler administrators, comparing each action to the condemning of a piece of private property to the use of the universe. When the canal connecting the Atlantic with the Pacific shall be completed, no more waterways uniting oceans will be necessary or possible. But, did a weak people possess a site that might be utilized by the ebbing and flowing of the globe's shipping, when a canal had been made, they would obviously hesitate a long time before voluntarily parading its advantages.

The uniting of the Mediterranean and Red seas was considered long before the birth of Christ, and many wise men and potentates toyed with the project in the hoary ages. The Persian king, Necho, was dissuaded sixteen hundred years before the dawn of Christianity from embarking in the enterprise, through the warning of his favorite oracle, who insisted that the completion of the work would bring a foreign invasion, resulting in the loss of canal and country as well. The great Rameses was not the only ruler of the country of the Nile who coquetted with the project. In 1800 the engineers of Napoleon studied the scheme, but their error in estimating the Red Sea to be thirty feet below the Mediterranean kept the Corsican from undertaking the cutting of a canal. Mehemet Ali, whose energies for improving the welfare of his Egyptian people were almost boundless, never yielded to the blandishment of engineers scheming to pierce the isthmus; he may have known of the prognostication of Necho's oracle.

Greater than any royal actor in the Suez enterprise, however, was Ferdinand de Lesseps, the Frenchman whom history persists in calling an engineer. By training and occupation he was a diplomatist, probably knowing no more of engineering than of astronomy or therapeutics. Possessing limitless ambition, he longed to be conspicuously in the public gaze, to be great. He excelled as a negotiator, and knew this; and it came easy to him to organize and direct. In his day the designation "Captain of Industry" had not been devised. In the project of canalizing the Suez isthmus—perennial theme of Cairo bazaar and coffee-house—he recognized his opportunity, and severed his connection with the French Consulate-General in Egypt to promote the alluring scheme, under a concession readily procured from Viceroy Saïd. This was in 1856.

Egypt had no debt whatever when Saïd Pasha signed the document. But when the work was completed, in 1869, the government of the ancient land of the Pharaohs was fairly tottering under its avalanche of obligations to European creditors, for every wile of the plausible De Lesseps had been employed to get money from simple Saïd, and later from Ismail Pacha, who succeeded him in the khedivate. For fully a decade the raising of money for the project was the momentous work of the rulers of Egypt; but more than half the cash borrowed at usurious rates stuck to the hands of the money brokers in Europe, let it be known, while the obligation of Saïd or Ismail was in every instance for the full amount.

Incidentally, a condition of the concession was that Egypt need subscribe nothing, and as a consideration for the concession it was solemnly stipulated that for ninety-nine years—the period for which the concession was given—fifteen per cent. of the gross takings of the enterprise would be paid to the Egyptian treasury.

Learning the borrowing habit from his relations with plausible De Lesseps, the magnificent Ismail borrowed in such a wholesale manner, for the Egyptian people and himself, that in time both were hopelessly in default to stony-hearted European creditors. Egyptian bonds were then quoted

PORT SAID ENTRANCE TO SUEZ CANAL, SHOWING DE LESSEPS'S STATUE

in London at about half their face value, and Britons held a major part of them.

England had originally fought the canal project, opposing it in every way open to her power and influence at Continental capitals. The belief in time dawning upon the judgment of Britain that the canal would be finished and would succeed, her statesmen turned their energies to checkmating and minimizing the influence of De Lesseps and his dupe Ismail. The screws were consequently put on the Sultan of Turkey—whose vassal Ismail was —resulting in that Merry Monarch of the Nile being deposed and sent into exile, and the national cash-box at Cairo was at the same time turned over to a commission of European administrators —and is yet in their keeping.

But the miserable people of Egypt, the burdened fellaheen, resented the interference of Christian money-lenders, demanding more than their pound of flesh. The Arabi rebellion resulted, when British regiments and warships were sent to quell the uprising and restore the authority of the Khedive. That was nearly a quarter of a century ago; but since the revolution the soldiers and civil servants of England have remained in Egypt, and to all intents and purposes the country has become a colony of England. The defaulted debts of the canal-building period were responsible for these happenings, be it said.

Verily, the fulfilment of Necho's oracle came with terrible force, and generations of Nile husbandmen must toil early and late to pay the interest on the public debt incurred through Ismail's prodigality. This degraded man in his exile persistently maintained that he believed he was doing right when borrowing for the canal, for it was to elevate Egypt to a position of honor and prominence in the list of nations. And it is the irony of fate, surely, that Ismail's personal holding in the canal company was sacrificed to the British government for half its actual value, on the eve of his dethronement, and that every tittle of interest in the enterprise held by the Egyptian government—including the right to fifteen per cent. of the receipts—was lost or abrogated. Owning not a share of stock in the undertaking, and having no merchant shipping to be benefited, Egypt derives no more advantage from the great Suez Canal than an imaginary kingdom existing in an Anthony Hope novel.

The canal has prospered beyond the dreams of its author; but this means no more to the country through which it runs than the success of the canals of Mars. De Lesseps died in a madhouse and practically a pauper, while Ismail spent his last years a prisoner in a gilded palace on the Bosporus, and was permitted to return to his beloved country only after death. These are but some of the tragic side-lights of the great story of the Suez Canal.

A few years since there was a movement in France to perpetuate De Lesseps's name by officially calling the waterway the Canal de Lesseps. But England withheld its approval, while other interests having a right to be heard believed that the stigma of culpability over the Panama swindles was fastened upon De Lesseps too positively to merit the tribute desired by his relatives and friends. As a modified measure, however, the canal administration was willing to appropriate a modest sum to provide a statue of the onco honored man to be placed at the Mediterranean entrance of the canal.

There stands to-day on the jetty at Port Saïd, consequently, a bronze effigy of the man for a few years known as "*Le grand Français,*" visage directed toward Constantinople (where once he had been potent in intrigue), the left hand holding a map of the canal, while the right is raised in graceful invitation to the maritime world to enter. This piece of sculpture is the onlymaterial evidence that such a person as Ferdinand de Lesseps ever lived. The legacy to his family was that of a man outliving his importance and fair name.

The name Port Saïd commemorates the viceroy granting the concession, while Ismail the Splendid has his name affixed to the midway station on the canal, Ismailia, where tourists scramble aboard the train bound for Cairo and the Nile. The actual terminus at the Suez end is called Port Tewfik, after Ismail's son and successor in the khedivate. This convenient mode of perpetuating the names of mighty actors in the Suez drama suggests a certain sentimentality, but the present generation cares as little for the subject as for a moldy playbill hanging in a dark corner of a club-house.

As an engineering feat the construction of the canal was nothing remarkable. Any youth knowing the principles of running lines and following the course of least resistance might have planned it. In Cairo and Alexandria it is flippantly said that De Lesseps traced with his gold-headed walking-stick the course of the canal in the sand, while hundreds of thousands of unpaid natives scooped the soil out with their hands. The work was completed with dredges and labor-saving machinery, as a fact. The enterprise cost practically $100,000,000—a million dollars a mile; and half this was employed in greasing the wheels at Constantinople and Paris. Probably the work could to-day be duplicated, by using machinery similar to that employed on the Chicago Drainage Canal, for $25,000,000. The task would be a digging proposition, pure and simple.

A cardinal article of faith of the legal status of the canal is its absolute internationality. By its constitution no government can employ it in war time to the exclusion or disadvantage of another nation. By a convention becoming operative in 1888 the canal is exempt from blockade, and vessels of all nations, whether armed or not, are forever to be allowed to pass through it in peace or time of war.

Critics of Britain's paramount interest in India and her aspirations in the Far East, nevertheless, pretend to see a decided advantage accruing from England's control of things Egyptian. They claim that Britain's position is immensely

ITALIAN WARSHIP STEAMING THROUGH CANAL

strengthened by the presence in Cairo and Alexandria, within a few hours' journey of the canal, of a half-dozen regiments of redcoats ready for any emergency. Another proof of England's interest in the great universal artery of travel is the maintaining of guard-ships at either terminus, which incidentally keep watchful eyes on the coal-bins of Suez and Port Saïd. A vessel unofficially sunk in an awkward position in the canal might delay for weeks the arrival of an unfriendly fleet in Asiatic waters.

The British government and British trade have fattened tremendously from the canal. Being the short-cut to England's treasure-house in the East, it is more or less equitable that Britain's flag flies over sixty per cent. of the canal traffic; and, fully as important, is the tremendous increase in value of the shares in the company held by the British government. It was in 1875 that Disraeli secured to his countrymen the permanent control of the canal through the purchase from embarrassed Ismail of that potentate's personal holding in the undertaking. This midnight negotiation, conducted over the cable, was Disraeli's most material triumph as a statesman. For $20,000,000 he purchased shares having now a market value of $135,000,000. A few hours after the consummation of this negotiation a group of French bankers, then in Cairo, seeking to acquire the shares, were amazed to learn that they had been outwitted. A well-posted newspaper correspondent at the French capital had informed Britain's ambassador of the purpose of the bankers' visit to Egypt—and astute Disraeli did the rest.

This transferred from France to her rival across the channel the right to direct the policy of De Lesseps's creation. But French susceptibilities have always been considered in matters connected with the conduct of the enterprise—it is still "La Compagnie Universelle du Canal Maritime de Suez," the tariff is based on French currency, the principal office is in Paris, and the official language of the company is French.

The world knows the Suez marine highway only in its utilitarian aspect, and America's interest therein is that attaching to it as an enterprise forerunning Uncle Sam's route at Panama. Before many years have passed the two canals will to some extent be rivals. The Suez cutting is practically ninety-nine miles in length, and at present 121 feet wide, with a depth accommodating craft drawing twenty-six feet and three inches. To handle modern battleships and the increasing size of cargo steamers, both depth and width are to be increased. Having no sharp curvatures, and excavated at a level from sea to sea, ships proceed by night assisted by electric lights with the same facility as by day. The time consumed in transit is from fourteen to eighteen hours. Not for a decade has a sailing vessel used the canal, and the widest craft ever traversing the canal was the dry-dock *Dewey,* sent under tow by the government from the United States to the Philippines. The tariff is now reduced to $1.70 per ton register, and

$2 for every passenger. A ship's crew pay nothing. The toll for a steamer of average size, like a Peninsular and Orient liner, is about $10,000. I first passed the canal in a yacht of the New York Yacht Club, for which the tax was $400, and the last time I made the transit was in a German-Lloyd mail steamer which paid $7,000 for tonnage and passengers.

The canal's value to the commerce of the world is sufficiently proved by the saving of distance effected by it, as compared with the route around the Cape of Good Hope. By the latter the distance between England and Bombay is 10,860 miles, by the canal 4,620 miles, and from New York to the leading ports of India the Cape route is about 11,500 miles, while by the canal the journey is shortened to 7,900 miles. How rapidly the traffic attracted by the economy in distance thus effected has developed, is best illustrated by the following statement, taken quinquennially from the company's returns:

Year	Steamers	Net Tonnage	Receipts in Francs
1871	765	761,467	7,595,385
1876	1,457	2,069,771	27,631,455
1881	2,727	4,136,779	47,193,880
1886	3,100	5,767,655	54,771,075
1891	4,206	8,699,020	83,421,500
1896	3,407	8,594,307	79,652,175
1901	3,699	10,823,840	100,386,397
1906	3,780	11,750,000	103,700,000

The Suez company pays enormously, and more than half the current earnings go to the possessors of the several grades of bonds and shares. Great Britain is the preponderating user of the canal, with Germany a poor second. Holland, due to proprietorship of Dutch India, is third in the list, and the nation of De Lesseps is fourth. The United States stands near the foot of the roll of patrons, being only represented by an occasional warship, transport going to or coming from the Philippines, or a touring yacht. It is a pathetic fact that our country, paramount producer of the world, has not been represented for nearly a decade by the Stars and Stripes over a commercial craft in the Suez canal. Cargoes go or come between American ports and those of the Orient, of course, but they are borne in British bottoms or those having register in other foreign nations. Fifteen or sixteen years ago England was represented in Suez statistics by seventy-five per cent. of the total traffic; but her proportion has decreased until it is now under sixty per cent. Kaiser William making a systematic fight for new markets in China and throughout Australasia, the statistics of Germany in canal traffic are slowly advancing.

At present, with the Suez enterprise in operation thirty-eight years, the average number of ships using the waterway is approximately ten each day. This is one vessel every two hours and thirty-five minutes during the twenty-four hours —meaning an eastbound craft every five hours and ten minutes, and a westbound every five hours and ten minutes.

The World's Turnstile at Suez

The idea of wedding the Atlantic and the Pacific must have been original with the first observant and intelligent person viewing the two oceans from the hills of the Central-American isthmus. Presumably he was a Spanish adventurer, and the time practically four hundred years ago. A century before the landing on American soil of the Pilgrim Fathers, explorers were informing Charles V of Spain of the opportunity supplied by nature to connect the waters of the two oceans. In 1550, one Galvao, a Portuguese navigator, wrote a book to prove the feasibility of an artificial connection between the Atlantic and the Pacific; and in 1780 a scientific commission from Spain studied the three Central-American routes—Panama, San Blas, and Nicaragua. These are simple facts to be pondered over by busy people who may possibly be in doubt as to whether the "father" of the isthmian enterprise was De Lesseps, Theodore Roosevelt, or Admiral Walker.

But it required a knowledge of practical geography to learn that from Colon to Panama by sea is eight thousand miles, instead of forty-seven across country—and it took a dauntless American President to demand that his government construct a national water route across the isthmus at Panama, and to point the way to that end; and this was done against potent opposition to any canal, and expressed preference of powerful statesmen for the unfeasible Nicaraguan project.

It may be profitable for enthusiasts jumping at

the conclusion that the American canal will pay from its opening, to study the returns of the Suez enterprise, the first full year of whose operation (1870) showed gross takings of only $1,031,365 from tolls levied upon 486 vessels. Speaking generally, a shipper sends his cargo by way of Suez only when 3,000 miles at least of ocean steaming may be saved—this is the approximate economy effected by the great turnstile between West and East, counting time, fuel, wages and other expenses. It may be accepted as a concrete fact that the employment of any canal by commerce must ever depend upon economic considerations.

Already acknowledging our commercial predominance, Europeans are not blind to the real purpose of the Panama Canal. But it should be borne in mind that whenever it is an open choice between the canal toll and the equivalent of time at sea, the Briton will be slow to decide in favor of contributing to the resources of a nation rising in brief time to commercial premiership; and Frenchmen, economists by nature, will take a similar view, as will Germans, and shippers of other nations. Expressed in the fewest words, the employment of the Panama route will be governed exclusively by self-interest, computed from the standpoint of material economy; sentimentality will bring not one ship to Uncle Sam as a patron —unless it be an American ship.

Suez will always be favored by European shipmasters determining routes for cargoes in which Panama and Suez present advantages practically equal; probably the expense of a few hundred miles additional travel would not cause them to break from the old route, by which there is no risk of accident or delay from canal-locks. A considerable percentage of the oversea carrying trade controlled by British bottoms is geographically independent of canals, and will always be. For example, the bulk of traffic to and from the west coast of South America—the rich nitrate trade of Iquique and Valparaiso—will not ordinarily be altered by the Panama Canal. The economy of distance from the latter port to England and the Continent by the canal being only about 1,500 miles, this traffic, except under unusual circumstances, will continue as long as it goes in British vessels to round the extremity of South America.

Singapore will be the Asiatic port differentiating the attracting power of the Panama and Suez canals, speaking from the basis of Atlantic and Gulf ports as points of origin or destination. Cargoes for places west of the 105th degree of east longitude will logically be sent through the Mediterranean and the Suez Canal. But the area east of the Singapore degree of longitude is teeming with opportunity for Panama cargoes. The isthmian short cut to Oceanica and Asia, comprising the coastal section of China's vast empire, enterprising Japan, the East Indies, Australia, New Zealand, and our own Philippine archipelago, is the world's most potential area. The awakened Orient can use American products to practically limitless extent. One third of the trade of these lands would make America great as a world-provider, and could be secured if we embarked seriously in an effort to obtain it. Students of economics have never admitted the logic of America's sending cotton to England to be there converted into fabrics clothing half the people of the East.

Let the reader, content in belief that our manufactures have an extensive use in the outer world, because America heads the list of exporting nations, investigate the subject, and his reward will be to learn that *we export only a trifle more than six per cent. of what we manufacture.* Let him also study the statistics of our commerce with South America, natural products and manufactures of every sort—they are replete with astonishing facts. To discover that our exports to the southern continent do not equal $2 per capita of South America's population will surprise the investigator, doubtless; and that the volume of trade is overwhelmingly with England and Germany will likewise be disconcerting. South America has 40,000,000 people; but Mexico's 13,500,000 inhabitants buy nearly as much from Uncle Sam as the South Americans. We now sell Canadians products averaging $30 per capita annually.

The reason for the startling disparity in the statistics of trade intercourse with our adjoining neighbors, Canada and Mexico, and oversea South America, is obviously the lack of transportation facilities under the American flag; and the adage that "trade follows the flag" has earned more significance than attaches to a mere figure of speech. We pay South America yearly, let it be known, about $120,000,000 for coffee, wool, hides and other raw products; and the major share of this money is expended in Europe for the necessities and luxuries of life. This is inequitable, to say the least, and should be remedied. Uncle Sam must look to the Orient, as well, and seek to make China his best customer. Every nation in Europe whose foreign trade is worth considering exploits foreign countries in the thorough manner of a great commercial house—getting business by the most productive, not the easiest, methods. In frequent magazine articles I have insisted that the isthmian canal, "destined to make the United States the trade arbiter of the world," could never be expected to "pay" directly. The artificial waterway is to cost a vast deal of money; with the payments to the French company and to the republic of Panama, added to the sum necessary to the completion of the work, Uncle Sam's expenditure cannot be less than $225,000,000! It will probably be more. A private incorporation embarked in the enterprise would hold that the investment was entitled to five per cent. interest, say, and in time be funded. The money of the nation, embarked in a project distinctly commercial, merits a reasonable rate of income or benefit—four per cent. certainly. To operate the canal with the expensive up-keep essential to a region of torrential rains, cannot be less than $4,000,000 annually; if the Chagres River refuses to be confined in bounds, the cost will be greater. The items of yearly expense figured here total $13,000,000—a sum to be regarded as the very minimum of the cost of maintaining and operating the canal.

Optimistic students of ocean transportation statistics say the canal will draw 10,000,000 tons of shipping a year; others, conservative of opinion, say half this volume. Taking the mean of these estimates, I hazard the statement that six years after the canal is opened, the tonnage will be 7,500,000. The Suez Canal was operated more than thirty years before its business aggregated 10,000,000 tons; and to attract this volume, several reductions in tolls were necessary. The American government cannot properly levy a heavier tribute at Panama than is demanded at Suez, for the fact is, our canal will not be as essential as that uniting Europe and the East. A like tariff would produce for Uncle Sam, on the hypothesis of a business of 7,500,000 tons, only $12,-750,000 a year; a higher tariff would probably produce less. And here is an unpalatable truthlet —Panama's earnings from passengers can never be considerable, compared with that constant ebbing and flowing of humanity between the home countries of Europe and their dependencies in Asia, Africa and Australasia. As a highway of travel, Panama can never have a quarter of the income from passengers as that yearly accruing to the Suez company. It may be unpopular to here record the opinion that the *direct* increment of the American canal cannot for many years yield

CARGO STEAMER IN THE CANAL AT KILOMETER 133

what in a commercial enterprise could be called a profit.

The way to compel the canal to pay *indirectly* is to make it incidental to the development of a mighty commercial marine, that will carry American products to present foreign markets, and to new markets, under the Stars and Stripes. This accomplished, the United States will indisputably be the trade arbiter of the universe. With operations under way on the isthmus, is not the time propitious for popular discussion throughout the nation, and in official Washington, how best to *create* the commerce that will make the Panama Canal a success from its opening?

We have populated the country, developed resources of field, forest and mine, and devised matchless ways of translating natural products into finished articles appealing to all mankind. Now, let us cease sending these products of soil and workshop to market in British ships; let us forward them in vessels constructed in American shipyards, thereby making the transaction independently American. Already have we produced ocean carriers equal to the best; while American war-ships, native from keel to topmast truck, are the envy of the world.

Not for a decade has a commercial vessel under the American flag passed the Suez Canal, I have stated. But the time was when Uncle Sam's ensign was the emblem oftenest seen in foreign harbors.

In but one department of natural growth is the

United States backward—shipping, in its broad and commercial acceptance. To promote it should now be the plan of both political parties.

Our canal can never pay until we enter as shipowners into competition with Europe's trading nations, and these possess a material interest in the Suez undertaking, be it remembered. The commercial fleet at present under the American flag could not pay a tenth of Panama's operating expenses. When we seriously embark upon the work of creating a great merchant marine, we are going to rouse spirited opposition. Englishmen, Germans, and Frenchmen will not like it; and Europeans cannot be expected to take any interest in the welfare of our national canal, and all may object to fattening the treasury of a country that is their trade competitor. These facts, insignificant as they may seem, prove in reality the need for supplying hundreds of ocean carriers under the same flag as that flying over the canal zone.

By the time the canal is opened, the United States will have 100,000,000 inhabitants; and agriculture, assisted by ordinary methods and by irrigation, will have developed to an extent making our commodities dictators of supply and price. By that time, sea transportation cannot be regarded as a competitor of transcontinental railway systems that have done much toward making the country what it is: water transportation will be found a necessary adjunct to rail facilities, relieving the roads of a fraction of their through traffic.

To restore the Stars and Stripes to the seas will

require years of earnest effort, much debating in the halls of Congress, a drastic liberalizing of marine laws, and much prodding of human energies by editorial writers.

Suez shareholders, when asked by Americans if they fear any rivalry from Panama, reply: "None at all; unless"—and here is the kernel of the matter—"your countrypeople find a way of creating a mercantile marine coincidently with the building of the canal."

With unlimited financial resources to promote the most gigantic of modern enterprises, with inexhaustible raw and cultivated products, with labor to produce any conceivable commodity, the humiliating fact confronted the people of the United States a few months since of seeing its official delegates to the Pan-American Congress at Rio de Janeiro set forth in a steamship flying the red flag of Great Britain.

The most remarkable accomplishment in the material history of the world is that the United States secured her commercial supremacy without possessing a merchant marine. It is one of the marvels of modern times, surely.

CHAPTER II

COLOMBO, CEYLON'S COSMOPOLITAN SEAPORT

A MODERN man of business might believe that Bishop Heber of Calcutta wove into irresistible verse a tremendous advertisement for Ceylon real estate, but repelled investors by a sweeping castigation of mankind, when he wrote:

> What though the spicy breezes
> Blow soft o'er Ceylon's isle;
> Though every prospect pleases,
> And only man is vile.

In tens of thousands of Christian churches the praises of Ceylon are thus sung every Sunday, and will be as long as the inhabitants of America and Great Britain speak the English language. Some of the divine's statements, to be acceptable as impartial testimony, require modification; for the natural charms of the island are not so sweepingly perfect, and there man is far above the Asian average. Hymnists, it may be inferred, write with some of the license of poets. No part of England's great realm, nevertheless, is more beautiful than the crown colony of Ceylon in the Indian Ocean.

THE JETTY AT COLOMBO

Colombo, Ceylon's Seaport

An Eastbound traveler during the long run from Aden hears much of the incomparable island of palms, pearls, and elephants; and every waggish shipmate haunts smoke room and ladies' saloon waiting for the opportunity to point out the lighthouse on Minecoy Island in the Maldives as "the Light of Asia." Four hundred miles further and your good ship approaches Colombo. The great breakwater, whose first stone was laid by Albert Edward, is penetrated at last, and the polyglot and universal harbor of call unfolds like a fan.

There's music within; the breezes bring proof of this. Surely, it is Bishop Heber's trite stanzas repeated in unison by the forgiving populace—they are sung everywhere, and why not in Ceylon's great seaport? The ship churns forward to her moorings. It is singing; there is no mistaking it. But the air? Does it deal with "spicy breezes," and "pleasing prospects?" No; it is a sort of chant. Listen again. Ah, it is Lottie Collins's masterpiece, not Bishop Heber's: it is "Ta-ra-ra boom de-ay." And the chanters are dozens of Britain's loyal subjects, youths naked and black, lying in wait to induce passengers to shower coins into the sea in recompense of a display of diving from catamarans constructed from trunks of palm-trees.

If asked what place in all the world can in a day show the greatest medley of humanity, I should pronounce in favor of the landing-jetty at Colombo. Scurrying ashore from ocean steamers in launches, in jolly-boats pulled by oars fashioned like huge mustard-spoons, or in outrigger canoes that glide rapidly, are representatives of every nation of the West, of China, of Japan—in fact, of every division of God's footstool having place in the list of nations. Being the great port of call and coaling station linking Occident, Orient and Australasia, a traveler naturally wants to inspect the place and stretch his legs on shore, while his ship is stocking with fuel to carry it to Aden, Singapore or to an antipodean port. Tiffin or dinner on *terra firma* is likewise coveted by the traveler with appetite jaded by weeks of sea-cooking. Ceylon's capital teems consequently with people hungry for a *table d'hote* meal, a 'rickshaw ride, and the indiscriminate purchase of rubbishing cats-eye and sapphire jewelry.

The conglomeration of people on the promenade floor of the jetty, watching voyagers come and go, would tend to make a student of anthropology lose his mind. Every variety of man of Ceylon, practically of every creed and caste of India, even of all Asia, is there, and a liberal admixture of Europeans as well.

Leaning over the hand-rail all humanity appears equal—for sight-seeing purposes, certainly. There are gentle Cingalese men with hair twisted into a knot on the back of the head and large shell comb on the crown, Tamil coolies and Hindus in profusion, of course. There are fat Parsees from Bombay, and Buddhist priests and monks in yellow togas, each armed with palm-leaf fan and umbrella, precisely as Gautama Buddha left his father's mansion to sow the religion worshiped by nearly a third of the people of the earth. A group of lascars, on leave from a P. & O. liner, look depreciatingly on nautical brethren from colder climes. There are Malays, as well, obsequious Moormen merchants, and haughty Afghans from beyond the "Roof of the World," as scholars call the Himalayas. Here and there are broad-chested Arabs from Aden way and the Persian Gulf, taking chances on the announcement of a pearl "fishery" by the government—divers, who may secure a gem of price in an hour's work, or may return home empty-handed. Their neighbors on the platform are seafarers coming with the embassy from the Sultan of the Maldive Islands, bringing to the governor of Ceylon the annual tribute sanctioned by custom, and the renewed assurances of loyalty to Edward VII. Close by them, and taking a profound interest in a group of European ladies stepping from a launch below, are three black girls in the garb of Catholic Sisters of Charity, whose chains and crucifixes are of unusual size.

With a conscious air of proprietorship of the British Empire, khaki-clad Tommy Atkins comes down the pier, attended by the inevitable fox terrier. Following close on his heels is a towering man of ebon complexion, with three stripes of ashes and the wafer of humility on his forehead. He is barefooted, and his solitary garment is a piece of cotton with which he has girded his loins; he is abundantly lacquered with cocoanut oil, to protect him from contracting a cold from the too rigorous "spicy breezes" of Lanka's isle. A stranger would say he was a penitent wayfarer of God, not worth the smallest coin of the East. In one hand he carries an overfilled valise, and in the other a sunshade of immaculate white: the initiated recognize him to be a chettie, easily worth lakhs of rupees, who is presumably embarking for Rangoon, and there to purchase a cargo of rice.

Hark! There is commotion and much noise at the jetty entrance. Can it be an alarm of fire, or have the customs officials at the gates apprehended a flagrant smuggler? Oh, no; it is merely Great Britain arriving on the scene in the person of a smart-looking tea-planter who has honked down in his motor-car to see a comrade off on the mail steamer; incidentally, some of the noise proceeds from a group of sailors on leave from a battleship who are wrangling with 'rickshaw men as to proper payment for having been hauled about the city on a sight-seeing tour. And so it goes in Colombo. Each day presents a picture not to be adequately described by a less gifted writer than Kipling.

Colombo is the westermost town of that great division of Asia wherein subject races—black, brown and yellow—haul the white man in jinrickshaws. No institution of the East stamps the superiority of the European more than this menial office of the native. Probably every American when brought face to face with the matter says manfully that he will never descend to employing a fellow creature to run between shafts like an animal, that he (visi-

HINDU SILVERSMITHS, COLOMBO

tor from a land where rights of mankind are equal and constitutional) may be spared from footweariness under a tropic sun. It is a noble impulse—but weak man is easily tempted. Hence, you decide to try the 'rickshaw just once.

The sensation is found to be agreeable, surprisingly so. Your fellow mortal, you perceive, is dripping with perspiration under the awful heat of the sun, while beneath the hood of the vehicle you are cool and comfortable. Then you yield to the savage defects of your moral make-up—and decide never to walk another yard in the East, not when a 'rickshaw is to be had. The habit comes as easily as drinking, or anything that your conscience and bringing-up tell you is not quite right, although enjoyable.

The 'rickshaw in Colombo is a splendid convenience. The runner's rights are as loyally protected as those of his employer, and he readily covers six miles an hour at a swinging gait. If his vehicle has rubber tires and ball-bearings the labor is not severe. The man might have a harder vocation with smaller pay.

Colombo has hotels that would satisfy in Europe or America—one, the Grand Oriental, is spoken of as the most comfortable hostelry between Cairo and San Francisco. To refer to it by its full name stamps the newcomer and novice at traveling—throughout half the world it is known familiarly as the "G. O. H." Two miles from Colombo, gloriously situated on the sea-front, the Galle Face Hotel is fashionable, cool and quiet, but lacking in the characteristic of being an international casino—which assuredly the "G. O. H." is. Tiffin or dinner is an interesting function at a Colombo hotel, for one never knows who or what his table mates may be. In the East every man who travels is assumed to be somebody. Hence you suspect your *vis-a-vis* at dinner to be the governor of a colony somewhere in the immeasurable Orient, or a new commander for Saigon, or perhaps a Frankfort banker going to China to conclude the terms of a new loan. If your neighbor at table is specially reserved, and gives his orders like one accustomed to being obeyed, you fancy him to be an accomplished diplomatist, very likely having in his pocket the draft of a treaty affecting half the people of the Far East. No one seems ever to suspect his confrères of being mere business men. And the ladies—well, they may be duchesses or dressmakers no longer content with traveling "on the Continong"; nobody cares which. If they are very well gowned, probably they are the latter.

An army of waiters clad in spotless and snowy uniforms with red facings and shining buttons set before you dishes you never heard of. Some are satisfying in the extreme; but these waiters, can they be described as in uniform? True, their garments are alike, but the head-gear is of infinite variety. According to caste or nationality each proclaims himself. But look once more; there *is* uniformity, for all are barefooted.

Wonderful fellows these Easterns. The native hotel band, led by a wandering European, plays

A HIGH PRIEST OF BUDDHA

Sousa's marches and "Hiawatha," yes, even "Tammany," with accuracy; and the cooks prepare dishes with French names, make *vin blanc* and *Hollandaise* sauces worthy of Delmonico or Ritz, and this without permitting the palate to guide them. If they tasted food concocted for Christians a million kinds of perdition might be their punishment. Music may be mechanical, as it is claimed to be, but not cooking. How do the gastronomic experts of pagan Asia acquire their skill?

Considering that the Ceylon capital is only four hundred miles north of the equator, the heat is never extremely oppressive. One's energies there, nevertheless, are not what they are farther north or at higher elevations. Kandy, the ancient up-country capital, is cooler, and Nuwara Eliya, in the mountains, is actually cold at night. When white people do anything in Colombo—work, attend church, play bridge, or billiards—a native keeps them moderately comfortable with swinging *punkahs.* Some hotels and residential bungalows have discarded punkahs for mechanical fans; but the complaint is that the electricity costs more than the *punkah-wallah*—the fan-boy of the East. "Ah, yes; but your wallah frequently falls asleep at his work," you remark to the resident. "True, and your electricity frequently fails us," is the reply.

Pear-shaped Ceylon, separated from India by only fifty miles of water, is three fourths the size of Ireland, and its population 3,600,000. Seventy-five per cent. of the people are Cingalese, and their language a dialect harking back to Sanskrit. The Cingalese are mostly Buddhists, with a sprinkling of Roman Catholics, the latter religion having been left in the land by its one-time Portuguese rulers. The Tamils, numbering a million, are not native to the island, like the Cingalese, but have come from southern India as laborers on coffee and tea estates; they are chiefly Hindus, although thousands have been converted to the Christian faith. The Mohammedan Moormen, living on the coast, approximate a quarter of a million in number. Europeans of all nationalities, not including the British troops, total only 6,500, a percentage of the island's human family to be computed in fractions.

The Cingalese seen chiefly in the towns wear their long hair arranged like a woman's, and around their heads a large, semicircular comb of shell, as has been said. The comb has nothing to do with religion or caste—contrary to what a visitor is usually told; it merely announces the wearer to be not of the coolie class, who carry sacks of rice and cases of merchandise on their heads. Half the people of Ceylon wear no headgear, and not two per cent. know what it is to wear shoes.

Colombo's population is about 160,000. The capital is a handsome city, with communities on seafront, on the shores of a sinuous lake, and ranging inland for miles through cinnamon gardens and groves of cocoanut-palms. Queen's

REPRESENTATION OF BUDDHA'S TOOTH, COLOMBO MUSEUM

House, where the governor resides, is a rambling pile. The general post-office is the best building in the capital, and the museum and Prince's club, close by, are entitled to notice. The hard red-soil roads of the city extend for miles into the palm forests, and are equal to any in the world. Government officials and European commercial people live in handsome suburban bungalows smothered amid superb foliage trees and flowering shrubs and vines.

What were called the maritime provinces of Ceylon were ruled by the Dutch until 1796. But in that year England supplanted Holland, and in 1815 she secured control of the entire island by overthrowing the Kandyan kingdom, for a long time confining European invasion to the island's seaboard. Ceylon costs Britain little worry and practically no expenditure. Strategically the island is valueless, save the benefit accruing to England in controlling if need be the enormous coal heaps of Colombo, and the maintenance there of a graving dock capable of handling the biggest battleship. Four hundred miles of government railways earn a tremendous profit, and moderate import and export duties on commodities keep the colonial cash-box well lined.

As in other Asiatic countries, the staple food is rice. Strange to say, Ceylon produces of this only half what is demanded by the people. Hence, it is necessary to import eight million bushels from India and Malay regions, costing approximately $5,000,000. On the other hand, the island sends to

Europe and America annually $21,000,000 worth of tea, besides considerable quantities of rubber, cocoanut-oil, cacao, and plumbago. Ceylon's crude rubber commands the highest price, and is a crop growing by leaps and bounds. It is estimated that eight hundred million cocoanuts are grown yearly in Ceylon. An item in the list of exports is elephants. These go to India as beasts of burden and pleasure, and the government collects two hundred rupees for every elephant sent from the island.

There is a possibility of two great events any springtime in Ceylon, and the prospect of either occurring is a theme of endless small talk in the offices and bungalow homes of everybody connected with "Government." One is the elephant kraal, planned for the edification of His Excellency the Governor and a few officials and visitors of distinction, who, from cages in trees at elevated points insuring safety, look down upon the driving in of converging herds of elephants. When an earth-strewn flooring of bamboo gives way and the monarchs of the jungle are cast into a stockaded pit, the kraal is complete. Then, ordinarily, the Ceylon treasury undergoes drafts for forage, until an authorized functionary negotiates the sale of the animals to maharajahs and lesser worthies up in India.

A kraal occurs every four or five years, or when a British royalty happens in Ceylon. Each governor is entitled by custom to the semi-royal honor at least once during his incumbency. The kraal is an enterprise usually paying for itself, unless there be a glut in the elephant market. The last kraal failed dismally, nevertheless, but for a very different reason. The drive had been so successful that the stockade was full to overflowing with leviathan beasts trumpeting their displeasure and wrath. While the dicker for their sale in India was proceeding, they became boisterously unruly, and, breaking down their prison of palm-tree trunks, scampered away to forest and jungle, without so much as saying "thank you" for weeks of gorging on rations paid for out of the public cash-box. And this was the reason why the kraal arranged for last year was abandoned, after hundreds of natives had been busy for weeks in "driving in" from every up-country district—to jeopardize good money was deemed not in keeping with the principles of good finance by certain material Britons responsible for the insular exchequer.

The popular event, coming as often as twice every three years, is the pearl-fishery. It interests everybody not living in mountain fastnesses, and appeals irresistibly to the hearts of the proletariat. Tricking elephants into captivity may be the sport of grandees, but the chance to gamble over the contents of the humble oyster of the Eastern seas invites participation from the meekest plucker of tea-buds on Ceylon's hill-slopes to the lowliest coolie in Colombo. Verily, the pearl-fishery is the sensational event of that land sung of by Bishop Heber.

CHAPTER III

THE LURE OF THE PEARL

THE bed of the Gulf of Manar, the arm of the Indian Ocean that separates Ceylon from India, has given the world more pearls than all other fisheries combined, for it has been prolific as a pearling-ground for thousands of years. Pearling in the gulf was an occupation hoary with age before the dawn of Christianity, for history tells us that Mardis, admiral of Alexander the Great, when returning from a voyage having to do with the Indian invasion, traversed the strait separating Ceylon from the continent, and was informed of the importance of the pearl-banks over which his fleet was passing. The great sailor was specially interested in the manner of drilling the holes in pearls for stringing, which was probably the same that it is to-day.

In the exuberant phraseology of the Orient, Ceylon is "the pearl-drop on India's brow," and the Gulf of Manar is "the sea abounding in pearls" and "the sea of gain." Ceylon appeals irresistibly to any possessor of the wandering foot, for it is an island paradise. It is well governed, of course, for its administration is that of a seasoned colony of Edward VII's realm, and the guidance of austere, dignified Britain countenances nothing like gambling in any of its lands—oh, dear, no! State lotteries are pretty well relegated in these times to Latin countries, everybody knows.

Yet the world's most gigantic gamble, pregnantly fruitful with chance in all variations and shadings, is unquestionably the Ceylon pearl-fishery; compared with it, any state lottery pales to insignificance. From the taking of the first oyster to the draining of the last vatful of "matter," every step is attended by fickle fortune; and never is the interest of the people of Portugal or of Mexico keener over a drawing of a lottery, the tickets of which may have been sold at the very thresholds of the cathedrals, than is that of the natives of Ceylon and southern India over the daily results of a Manar fishery.

Each bivalve is a lottery ticket; it may contain a gem worthy of place in a monarch's crown, or be a seed pearl with a mercantile value of only a few rupees. Perhaps one oyster in a hundred contains a pearl, and not more than one pearl in a hundred, be it known, has a value of importance. Nature furnishes the sea, pearling-banks, oysters, and all therein contained; the Ceylon administration conducts the undertaking, and for its trouble and trifling outlay exacts a "rake-off" of two thirds of all that may be won from the deep. And mere man, the brown or black diver, receives for his daring and enterprise one oyster in every three that he brings from the ocean's depths—and his earnings must be shared with boat-owner, sailors, attendants, and assistants almost without number.

For size of "rake-off," there is no game of hazard in the world offering a parallel. The Ceylon government used to exact three out of every four oysters brought in, the current tribute of two out of three having become operative only a few years since.

It should be known that the pearl-bearing oyster of the Indian Ocean is only remotely related to the edible variety of America and Europe. It is the *Margaritifera vulgaris*, claimed to belong to the animal kingdom, and not to the fish family, and is never eaten. The eminent marine biologist in the service of the Ceylon government, Professor Hornell, F. L. S., who intimately knows the habits of the pearl-oyster of the East, advances two interesting if not startling premises. One is that the pearl is produced as a consequence of the presence of dead bodies of a diminutive parasitical tapeworm which commonly affects the Ceylon bivalve. The living tapeworm does not induce pearl formation. The popular belief has been that the pearl was formed by secretions of nacre deposited upon a grain of sand or other foreign particle drawn within the oyster through its contact with the sea's bottom. The other Hornell assertion is that the oyster goeth and cometh at its pleasure; that it is mobile and competent to travel miles in a few weeks.

Scientists have long been aware that the pearl

MAP OF THE GULF OF MANAR, "THE SEA ABOUNDING IN PEARLS"

shell-fish possesses locomotive powers, which it uses when in quest of food or protection, and to escape impure localities. During the Dutch occupation of Ceylon, for example, there was a period of several years when the oysters' boycott of the Manar banks was virtually unanimous.

It is an accepted fact that pearls are excretions of superimposed concentric *laminæ* of a peculiarly fine and dense substance, consisting in major part of carbonate of lime. Linnæus, believing in the possibility of producing pearls by artifice, suggested the collecting of mussels, piercing holes in their shells to produce a wound, and bedding them for five or six years to give pearls time to grow. The Swedish government succeeded in producing pearls of a sort by this process; but as they were of trifling value, the experiments were discontinued.

Cunning Chinese and Japanese have sought of late years to assist or improve on nature's pearl-making methods by inserting tiny shot or grains of sand between the mantle and the shell, which in time become coated with nacre. Not long since there was a movement in Japan to embark in pearl production upon a basis wholly commercial, and its promoters discussed it as they might a project for supplying a city with vegetables. One of the claims of those exploiting the venture was that they could keep pace with fashion's changes by supplying pearls of any shape, pear, oval, or spherical. This has been accomplished in other countries, and European and American dealers have had years of acquaintance with the "assisted" pearl, a showy and inexpensive counterfeit, but one attaining to no position in the realm of true gems. The distinction between fine pearls and these intrusive nacre-coated baubles, alluringly advertised as "synthetic pearls," has been demonstrated by more than one devotee of science.

There are definite rules for determining when a Ceylon fishery will be held, for twice a year the banks are systematically examined by the marine biologist, and estimates made of the number of oysters present on each bank. Whenever their age and size appear to warrant the step, a sample catch of twenty thousand oysters is made by divers employed by the government, and a valuation is formed of the pearls they produce. If found to average ten or twelve rupees[1] to a thousand oysters, the government is advised to proclaim a fishery. Advertisements are then published throughout the East, especially in vernacular papers reaching the Persian Gulf and the two coasts of southern India, at the instance of the colonial secretary's office at Colombo. These detail the valuation of the sample pearls, area of beds to be fished, and the estimated number of oysters likely to be available upon each. The advertisements are printed in Cingalese, Tamil, and English. As rapidly as information can spread, it becomes known from Karachi to Rangoon, and along the chain of

[1] The rupee of India and Ceylon is equal to 32 cents U. S. A lakh is 100,000.

seaports of the Malay states, that a fishery is to be held. Divers, gem-buyers, speculators, money-lenders, petty merchants, and persons of devious occupations, make speedy arrangements for attending. Indian and Ceylon coolies flock by the thousand to the coast of the Northern province, longing to play even humble rôles in the great game of chance. The "tindals" and divers provide boats and all essential gear for the work afloat; while ashore the government supplies buildings and various forms of labor for dealing with the curious industry.

It is during the calm period of the northeast monsoon,—February, March and April,—when the sea is flat and the sky is bright and unflecked, that the fishery is carried on. The line of banks—they are "paars," in the languages of Ceylon—cover an extensive submarine plateau off the island's northwest coast, from ancient Hippuros southward to Negombo. This is of flat-surface rock, irregularly carpeted with coarse sand, and dotted with colonies of millions of oysters. Dead coral and other products of the sea are scattered everywhere on this plateau, and it is a theory that these surface interruptions prevent overcrowding of the oysters, and consequently assist in the bivalve's reaching the pearl-producing stage. It is claimed that a crowded paar contributes to a stunting of growth, bringing disease and premature death to the oyster, and consequently no pearls of account.

The estimate of the experts upon which it was

decided to announce a fishery last year was that there were on the Southwest Cheval paar 3,500,000 oysters which might be gathered, on the Mideast Cheval paar 13,750,000 oysters, on the North and South Moderagam 25,750,000, and on the South Cheval 40,220,000.

The announcement of this total of 83,000,000 bivalves produced an electrical effect, and an unprecedented attendance, for it was equal to announcing a lottery with that many tickets, and who knows how few prizes!

The student seeking to determine the eighth wonder of the world should not overlook the city of Marichchikkaddi. Stories of towns rising overnight wherever gold is found, or diamonds discovered, or oil struck, have become common to the point of triteness. Tales of the uprising of Klondike and South African cities, once amazing, fade to paltriness in the opinion of one who has seen the teeming city of Marichchikkaddi. In a sense it is a capital, yet it is found in no geography; no railway connects it with the world, yet a dozen languages are spoken in its streets. Marichchikkaddi's population numbers no young children, no persons too aged to toil, and the four or five hundred women sojourners merit the right of being present through serving as water-carriers to camp and fishing fleet.

This place with double-mouthful name, almost defying pronunciation, is the pearl metropolis of the universe. Probably there is not a stocked jewel-case that does not contain gems that have

COOLIES CARRYING PEARL OYSTERS FROM THE BOATS TO THE "KOTTU," OR GOVERNMENT STOCKADE

been filtered through this unique city by the sea. For a dozen reasons it is a wonderful town, and the foremost of these is that it is the only city of size that comes and goes like the tide's ebbing and flowing.

When a fishery is proclaimed, Marichchikkaddi is only a name—a sand-drifted waste lying between the jungle of the hinterland and the ocean. Yet nine months before forty thousand people dwelt here under shelter of roofs, and here the struggle for gain had been prosecuted with an earnestness that would have borne golden fruit in any city in the Western world. There, where lies the skeleton of a jackal half-buried in sand, an Indian banker had his habitat and office only a few months before, with a lakh of rupees stacked in a conspicuous place as glittering earnest of his ability to pay well for anything remarkable in the way of a pearl. And beyond, where occurs the rift in the sand, stood the shanty in which venturesome divers whiled away time and money in trying to pitch rings upon the ends of walking-sticks, as do farmers' boys at New England county fairs.

With the license permitting the calling of a pile of buildings formed of stucco a "White City," this metropolis might with propriety be named the "City of Brown," or, better, the "Cadjan City." For inaccessibility, it is in a class by itself.

Colombo is facetiously spoken of by Englishmen as the Clapham Junction of the East, for the reason that one can there change to a steamer carrying him virtually to any place on the globe.

But it is simpler for a white man to get to Melbourne, or Penang, or New York, from Colombo, than to obtain passage to Marichchikkaddi, only a hundred and fifteen miles up the coast. If he can wait long enough, passage may be found, of course; but otherwise all the official and editorial persuasion of Colombo—and the subsidized influence of the head porter of the "G. O. H.," availeth nothing. Now and then he may hear of a speculative Parsee's dhow that may be going to Manar for a cargo of shell-cased lottery tickets, or of a native-owned launch that will carry a limited number of passengers at an unlimited fare. A fast-sailing outrigger canoe may always be chartered. Another opportunity is to travel two days by post-cart to a village one never heard of, transferring there to a bullock hackery that may take him through jungle roads to the cadjan metropolis—provided he is able to give instructions in Tamil, or a college-bred coolie can be found who knows English. Still another way is to take the semi-weekly steamer from Colombo to Tuticoriu, in southern India, then zigzag about the continent of Asia until he makes Paumben. Then it is a matter of only a few days when there will be a boat crossing to the pearl-camp. This is the surest way of getting to Marichchikkaddi; but it is like making the journey from New York to Boston by way of Bermuda.

Ceylon's substitute for virtually everything elsewhere used in the construction of buildings is the cadjan: it is at once board, clapboard, shingle, and lath. Cadjans are plaited from the leaf of the cocoanut- or date-palm, and are usually five or six feet long and about ten inches wide; the center rib of the leaf imparts reasonable rigidity and strength. Half the shelters for man and beast throughout the island are formed of cadjans, costing nothing but the making, and giving protection from the sun and a fair amount of security from the elements. The frame of a house is made of stakes planted in the ground, with rafters and beams resting in crotches conveniently left by the wood-cutter. This slender frame is covered with cadjans, arranged systematically, and sewn together with cocoanut-leaf strands or tender rattans. Not a nail is used, and cadjan flaps that may be raised or lowered from within the building take the place of glazed windows. A dwelling of this character, carpeted with palm-mats, and flanked with verandas, brings a flowing measure of comfort to the dweller in the tropics; but the gales of the annual southwest monsoon play havoc with cadjan roofs and walls.

It being known that a fishery will bring together at least forty thousand souls, a small army of coolies hastens to Marichchikkaddi a few weeks prior to the announced date for opening the fishery, to prepare the buildings necessary to house all and sundry, and to erect bungalows for the British functionaries having the enterprise in charge. Public buildings almost pretentious in size and design rise from the earth in a few days, including a residence for the governor of Ceylon, who is expected to grace the fishery by a visit; one for the government agent of the province in which the interesting industry is carried on; and another for the delegate of the Colonial Office. There rise, mushroom-like, as well, a court-house, treasury, hospital, prison, telegraph-office and post-office, and a fair example of that blessing of the East known as a rest-house, each reflecting surprising good taste, and being adequate to its purpose, and presumably completed at a cost well within the appropriation. Jerry-builders and grafters have yet to be discovered in Ceylon.

Marichchikkaddi parades structures dedicated neither to religion nor dissipation. But the bazaar-like alleys branching from the thoroughfares of the Cadjan City purvey many things not obtrusively obvious to the British official. Whatever his faith, the disciple of the pearl may solitarily prostrate himself beneath a convenient palm-tree, with face turned toward Mecca, or on the sea-front indulge the devotions stamping him a Hindu of merit.

In an administrative sense the important building is the "Kachcherie"—mayor's office and superintendent's headquarters in one; but the structure of material interest is the "kottu," wherein every sackful of oysters taken from the boats is counted and apportioned between the government and the divers. It is a parallelogram enclosure of two or three acres in area, fenced with bamboo palings, and roofed here and there to protect the coolies from the sun. For convenience, one end is as near the sea as prudence will admit; and the other, the official end, where accountants and armed guards are in command, is not far from the governmental offices. A system perfected by years of experience makes thieving within the kottu virtually impossible, and the clerks who record the count of oysters, and issue them upon official order, might safely conduct a bankers' clearing-house. On occasions they handle without error more than three million oysters in a day.

A quarter of a mile from the official section of the city is the great human warren and business region, where black men and brown—Hindus, Mohammedans, Buddhists, and the East's flotsam of religions—dwell and traffic in peaceful communion. A broad thoroughfare, starting from the edge of the plateau overlooking the sea and extending inland until the settlement yields to the open country, is the "Main street"; and here, for ten or twelve weeks, is one of Asia's busiest marts. This part of Marichchikkaddi is planned with careful regard for sanitary needs and hygiene. Streets cross at right angles, and at every corner stands a lamp-post rudely made from jungle wood, from which suspends a lantern ingeniously fashioned from an American petroleum tin. Sites on the principal streets are leased for the period of the fishery to persons proving their purposes to be legitimate. For a good corner lot perhaps twenty feet square the government receives as much as a thousand rupees; and a few hours after the lease is signed up goes a cadjan structure—

and a day later pearls worth a king's ransom may there be dealt in with an absence of concern astounding to a visitor.

Can these Easterners, squatting on mats like fakirs in open-front stalls, judge the merits of a pearl? Yes, decidedly. In the twinkling of an eye one of them estimates the worth of a gem with a precision that would take a Bond Street dealer hours to determine. The Indian or Cingalese capitalist who goes with his cash to Marichchikkaddi to buy pearls is not given to taking chances; usually he has learned by long experience every "point" that a pearl can possess, knows whether it be precisely spherical, has a good "skin," and a luster appealing to connoisseurs. A metal colander or simple scale enables him to know to the fraction of a grain the weight of a pearl, and experience and the trader's instinct tell him everything further that may possibly be known of a gem. It would be as profitless to assume to instruct an Egyptian desert sheikh upon the merits of a horse as to try to contribute information to the pearl-dealer of the East.

The calm period of the northeast monsoon is gentleness itself by the middle of February, and the Gulf of Manar is seldom more than rippled by its zephyrs. The fishery begins then. For weeks the divers have been arriving by craft of every conceivable type and rig. They are the aristocrats of the camp, and as they roam bazaars and streets or promenade the sea-front they are admired by coolies and peons as bull-fighters would be in Spain.

THE LATE RANA OF DHOLPUR IN HIS PEARL REGALIA

This Indian prince is said to have owned pearls valued at seven and a half millions of dollars, the accumulation, perhaps, of his ancestors during several centuries

Sturdy fellows they are, lithe of limb and broad of chest. Each brings a tangle of pots and kettles, bags and bales, but wears nothing throughout the fishery save a loin-cloth and now and then a turban denoting nationality or caste. There were forty-five hundred of them in 1905, and those from the Madras Presidency were the backbone of the enterprise. Nearly half the divers were registered from Kilakari, and hundreds came from the tip end of India. The men from Tuticorin were of the Parawa caste, and those hailing from Paumben were Moormen. The only Ceylon city contributing divers was Jaffna, whose men were of the fisher caste, said to be descendants of Arabs who settled sixty years ago at Jaffna. The divers coming the greatest distance were the negroes and Arabs from Aden and the Persian Gulf, most of whom landed at Colombo from trading steamers, and made their way by small boat or bullock hackery to the Cadjan City. These fellows have few equals as divers, but the administrative officers of the camp always fear that they will come into conflict with the police or launch a war in the name of Mohammed against the Hindus or Cingalese. Consequently, only a limited number are allowed to take part in the fishery.

An amusing incident was furnished last season by the arrival of a diver of some renown in India, who had participated profitably in several fisheries. Accompanied by his "manduck," the fellow had crossed from Paumben as a deck passenger on a British India steamer. When the vessel was anchored, the diver summoned a rowboat to take himself and traps ashore. Wearing nothing but loin-cloth and turban, the man descended the side-steps an example of physical perfection, and so thoroughly smeared with cocoanut butter that he shone like a stove-polish advertisement The boat grounding on the shelving bottom a hundred feet from shore, this precious Indian, who was to pass a good share of the ensuing ten weeks in the water, even at the bottom of the sea, deliberately seated himself astride the shoulders of his manduck, and was borne to dry land with the care of one whose religion might forbid contact with water. He carried beneath one arm throughout the trip from the small boat a gingham umbrella, and under the other an Indian railway guide.

There are neither wharves nor landing-stages at Marichchikkaddi. Even His Excellency the Governor must lay aside his dignity in going from his boat to the shore. The horde of people working about the pearling fleet, amphibious by nature, have little need for those accommodations and necessities which the commercial world call "landing facilities."

The world over, gambling and speculation are joined in many ways to superstition; and the Eastern diver is superstitious to the hour of his death. At Marichchikkaddi he devotedly resorts to the mystic ceremony of the shark-charmer, whose exorcism for generations has been an indispensable preliminary to the opening of a fishery. The shark-charmer's power is believed to be hereditary. If one of them can be enlisted on a diver's boat, success is assured to all connected with the craft. The common form of fortune-tempting nowadays is for a diver to break a cocoanut on his sinking-weight just before embarking. If it be a clean and perfect break, success is assured; if irregular and jagged, only ordinary luck may be anticipated; and if the shell be broken in without separating into halves, it spells disaster, and the alarmed fisher probably refuses to go with the boat.

Last year's fleet was the largest ever participating in a Ceylon fishery, three hundred and twenty boats being enrolled. The largest boats came from Tuticorin, and carried thirty-four divers each. The smallest boat had a complement of seven divers. Each diver was faithfully attended by a manduck, who ran his tackle and watched over his interests with jealous care both in and out of the water. Besides the manducks, every boat had numerous sailors, food- and water-servers, and a riffraff of hangers-on. It was estimated that divers and manducks aggregated nine thousand souls. A system of apportionment gives every man in a boat an interest in the take, the divers generally retaining two thirds of the bivalves granted them by the government rule controlling the fishery. The Kilakari divers observe a time-honored custom of giving to their home mosque the proceeds of one plunge each day.

Nature obligingly assists the workers on the banks by supplying a gentle off-shore breeze at daybreak, which sends the fleet to the fishing ground, six or eight miles from the shore. By two o'clock in the afternoon a gun from a government vessel directs the boats to set sail for the return. By this hour the breeze is accommodatingly from the sea, and the fleet runs home with flowing sheets. Navigation, it will be seen, plays a very subordinate part in Marichchikkaddi's marine enterprise.

With the exception of the divers from the Malabar coast, who plunge head foremost from a spring-board, the men go into the water in an upright position, and are hurried in their journey to the bottom by a stone weighing from forty to fifty pounds. Each diver's attendant has charge of two ropes slung over a railing above the side of the boat: one suspends the diving-stone, and the other a wide-mouthed basket of network. The nude diver, already in the sea, places the basket on the stone and inserts one foot in a loop attached to the stone. He draws a long breath, closes his nostrils with the fingers of one hand, raises his body as high as possible above water, to give force to his descent, and, loosening the rope supporting the weight, is carried quickly to the bottom. An Arab diver closes the nostrils with a tortoise-shell clip, and occasionally a diver is seen whose ears are stopped with oil-saturated cotton. The manduck hoists the weight from the bottom and adjusts it for the next descent. Meanwhile, the diver, working face downward, is filling the basket with oysters with speed. When the basket is filled or breath exhausted, the diver signals, and is drawn

INDIAN PEARL MERCHANTS READY FOR BUSINESS

up as rapidly as possible by the rope attached to the basket, and a specially agile diver facilitates the ascent by climbing hand over hand on the line When a man has been in the water half an hour, and made perhaps seven or eight descents, he clambers aboard the boat for a rest and a sunbath, and in a few minutes is taking part in the interminable chatter of the Orient.

A diver coming up with basket filled wears a face of benign contentment; but when the oysters are few and far between, as they are oftentimes, and the man has prolonged his stay below to the limit of his air supply, his head is out of water not many seconds before he is volubly denouncing the official control forcing him to work on a "paar" where little but sand exists, and his confrères on the boat hurl savage invective at any government functionary within earshot.

The powerful Eastern sun illumines the bottom sufficiently for a diver to plan his operations before going down, and nine days out of ten the overhead sun renders the sea sufficiently transparent to guide a boat's crew to promising anchorages. Pearling economists insist that dredging by machinery or the use of diving-suits can never compete with the simple and inexpensive method in vogue on the Manar banks. At Marichchikkaddi one hears frequent discussion of the time a diver may stay under water, and many improbable accounts of what has been done are told a visitor. An average Tamil or Moorman stays down not longer than forty-five seconds, while the broad-chested Arab thinks nothing of being under water from sixty to eighty seconds.

Depth has much to do with the time, and it is admitted that divers do not suffer unduly from the trying nature of their calling except when forced to work in unusually deep water. Seven or eight fathoms—about the average on the Ceylon banks—produces no injurious effect, but nine fathoms tell on all but men of sturdy build. Occasionally a declivity perhaps ten fathoms below the surface has to be fished, and this demands the service of picked men, divers possessing the highest vitality. Several divers collapse every season through toiling at unusual depths, and two or three pay the penalty of death. Most divers, however, live to as full a span as men pursuing other humble callings.

When a fishery is at its height, the scene on the banks is one of extreme animation, and a picture full of strangeness to New World eyes. Each craft is a floating hive of competitive noise and activity, and the center of a cordon of disappearing and reappearing seal-like heads, with baskets splashing in the water or being hauled by excited hands. In the distance floats the majestic barque *Rengasamy Puravey,* an old-timer, with stately spars, a quarter-deck, and painted port-holes that might cause a landsman to believe her a war-ship. For half the year the barque is the home of the government's marine biologist, and his office and laboratory, wherein scientific investigation and experimentation are in constant progress, are in houses built on the quarter-deck. Small steamers, having an official cut, move here and there among the fishing boats, doing patrol duty and carrying instructions when necessary from the *Rengasamy Puravey.*

"Would you like to go down in a diving-costume from a boat alongside the barque?" asks the biologist; "it 's perfectly safe, and I have a dress that will fit you. Frequently I go to the bottom to study the curious growths there, and last season the colonial secretary did the thing two or three times."

With a readiness of speech rivaling gunfire in promptness I nipped in the bud the preparations for carrying out the proffered courtesy, explaining that I was glad to accept a vicarious description of things at the ocean's bottom.

The dingy fleet blossoms into a cloud of canvas, with every boat headed for Marichchikkaddi, the instant the "cease work" gun is fired. The scene suggests a regatta on a gigantic scale, and from a distance the leaning lug and lateen sails of the East give the idea of craft traveling at terrific speed. It is a regatta, a free-for-all, devil-take-the-hindmost affair. The prizes are choice berths on the beach as near as possible to the kottu, and the coolies who must carry the sacks of oysters see to it that the "tindal" and his sailors make no retarding error.

The camp had been peaceful and somnolent while the boats were out; but the word that the fleet was coming in had roused every laborer, every petty dealer, speculator, and harpy to nervous activity. Everybody goes to the sea-front to witness the beaching of the boats and to watch the unloading. An hour probably elapses between the coming of the leader of the fleet and the arrival of the slowest boat. During this period the important functionary is the beach-master, who shouts his commands to boats seeking to crowd into positions not rightly theirs. When a boat is securely drawn upon the strand, there is no waste of time in getting the cargo started for the government storehouse. Muscular porters, glistening in their perspiring nudeness, go in single file between boat and kottu like ants executing a transportation feat. In a very few minutes the oysters are being counted by nimble-handed coolies. Important gamblers in oysters, men with sharp eyes and speculative instincts, have only to note the number of sacks delivered from one or two boats—and secure a hint from an obliging diver as to whether the bivalves are "thin" or "thick"—to arrive at a safe hypothesis of what the day's take has been, and also whether the oysters promise to be fairly pearliferous. The opinions of two or three of these experts make a basis for starting the prices at the auction in the evening, and these "sharps" are seldom wrong in their estimate of what would be a safe offer for a thousand chances in the great lottery of Asia.

The count in the kottu is soon completed, and each boat's catch is divided into three piles, when an official selects two for the government, and the third is so expeditiously removed that a quarter of an hour later the share of the divers is being huckstered throughout the camp to small speculators.

Upon each craft throughout the day has been a native watchman of supposed honesty, in the government's employ, whose duty has been to see that no oysters were surreptitiously opened on the banks or during the run home. Suspicion of the extraction of pearls on the part of any member of the crew leads to the police being informed, and an arrest follows. A favorite way of hiding pearls is to tie the gems in a rag attached to the anchor that is thrown overboard when the boat lands. Another is to fasten a packet to a piece of rigging adroitly run to the masthead, there to remain until opportunity permits the dishonest schemer to remove it unobserved.

On their way to their sleeping quarters it is interesting to observe divers stopping at boutiques and tea saloons for refreshments, paying their score with oysters, extremely acceptable to the shopkeeper itching to test his luck. In a small way, oysters pass current in the Cadjan City as the equivalent of coins. Probably the variations in value lead to fluctuations in exchange, but these are so keenly understood that the quotations are apparently adjusted automatically, like exchange between nations.

The sale is held in the building where the camp magistrate all the afternoon has been dispensing justice in breaches of Marichchikkaddi's morals—

simple assaults, thieving, and other petty misdemeanors usual to police courts. Punctually at sunset the auction begins. If the universe offers a stranger gathering for which commerce is responsible, it would be difficult to give it location. The gentle government agent sits on the platform, and in front of the rostrum is the splendidly appareled chief mudiliyar, to interpret between auctioneer and buyers. The bidders-to-be number half a hundred, and their eager faces are directed toward the august official of the government, each probably praying secretly to his god that undue competition be not inspired to the extent of excluding bargains. In the throng are chetties, Moor merchants, and local hawkers, hoping to get a few thousand bivalves at a price assuring a profit when peddled through the coastwise villages.

"Do these men represent actual capital?" you ask the agent. "They do, indeed," is the reply, "and collectively they are backed by cash in hand and satisfactory credits in Ceylon banks of at least a hundred lakhs of rupees." Forced as you are to accept the statement, you inwardly confess that they don't look it, for $3,200,000 is a goodly credit anywhere.

In the fading light of day the agent announces that approximately two million oysters are to be sold, and he invites offers for them by the thousand—the highest bidder to take as many as he chooses, the quotation to be effective and apply to others until it is raised by some one fearing there will not be oysters enough to satisfy the demands of everybody. It is the principle of supply and demand reduced to simplicity. The competition to fix the price of the first lot consumes perhaps a minute. The initial bid was thirty rupees; this was elevated to thirty-two, and so on until thirty-six was the maximum that could be induced from the motley assemblage. With his pencil the agent taps the table, and the mudiliyar says something in Hindustani meaning "sold." The buyer was an Arab from Bombay, operating for a syndicate of rich Indians taking a flier in lottery tickets. In a manner almost lordly he announces that he will take four hundred thousand oysters. Then a sale of two thousand follows at an advanced price to a nondescript said to have come all the way from Mecca; a towering Sikh from the Punjab secures twenty thousand at a reduced rate, and so on. In ten or twelve minutes the day's product is disposed of to greedy buyers for the sum of 62,134 good and lawful rupees. 'A clerk records names of buyers with expedition, glancing now and then at a document proving their credit, and in a few minutes issues the requisitions upon the kottu for the actual oysters that will be honored in the early morning.

The primitive process by which the pearls are extracted from the oysters is tedious, offensive to the senses, and of a character much too disagreeable to be associated with the jewel symbolizing purity. A few million oysters are shipped to southern India, and some go to Jaffna and Colombo; but the preponderating bulk is dealt with in the private kottus in the outskirts of the camp belonging to the men who crowd the auction room. To open fresh from the sea and scrutinize every part of the oyster would be too slow a method to be applied to the business of pearl-getting. The native who obtains a few dozen seeks shelter under the first mustard-tree, and with dull-edged knife, dissects each bivalve with a thoroughness permitting nothing to escape his eye.

The burning sun, bringing putrefaction and decay to the oyster, is the operator's agency for securing what pearls his purchase may contain. For a week or ten days the oysters are stacked in his private kottu, and the process of disintegration is facilitated by swarms of flies and millions of maggots. When the tropical sun can do no more, the contents of the shells—putrid, filthy, and overpoweringly odoriferous—are gathered in troughs and other receptacles to be put through a process of cleansing by washing with water frequently drawn away. The residue, carefully preserved, is picked over when dry by experts, working under the watchfulness of owner or his deputy—and in this manner the pearls of my lady's dainty necklace and the engagement ring are wrested from nature.

Sometimes an impatient speculator is seen with his coolies on the beach carefully washing vatfuls of "matter," perhaps employing a dugout canoe as a washing trough. Wherever the work is done the stench is almost overpowering, and the odors defy neutralization. The wonder is that some

THE LATE MAHARAJAH OF PATIALA IN HIS PEARL REGALIA

dread disease of the Orient does not make a clean sweep of the city's population. The medical officers claim that the malodorous fumes are not dangerous, and experience has taught these officials to locate the compounds, wherein millions of oysters are to decompose, in positions where the trade winds waft the smells seaward or inland, without greatly affecting the camp's health. The British official whose olfactory organ survives a season at the pearl camp deserves from his home government at least the honor of knighthood.

Interesting as Marichchikkaddi is to the person making a study of the conduct of unusual industries and the government of Eastern people, the medical officer looms important as the functionary shouldering a greater responsibility than any other officer of the camp. To draw forty thousand people from tropical lands, grouping them on a sand plain only a few hundred miles above the equator, is an undertaking pregnant with danger, when considered from the standpoint of hygiene. Strange to say, Marichchikkaddi's health is always satisfactory; but tons of disinfectants have to be used. Malarial fever is ever present, but is of a mild type. The outdoor dispensary does a rushing business, but only seventy-five cases were sufficiently serious last season to be sent to hospital, and only ten of these were fatal. The divers are prone to pneumonia and pleurisy, and these diseases carried off five. The deaths out of hospital totaled twenty-two.

In the hospital I saw a man with grizzled beard

whose escape from death bordered upon the marvelous. His head had been jammed four days before between colliding boats, cracking his skull to the extent of lettiug the brain protrude. He was rushed to the hospital to die, but had no intention of passing to another world, the doctors learned. Sitting upright on his cot-bed, the poor fellow said to me with an earnestness almost compelling tears: "Help me to get out of this place, please. I want to be with my boat, for there is no better diver than I am, and I can earn a hundred rupees a day as easily as any man in Marichchikkaddi."

As an illustration of the white man's supremacy, in dealing with black and brown peoples, Marichchikkaddi probably has no equal. Here, in an isolated spot on the coast of Ceylon, hours from anywhere by sea, and shut off from the large towns of the island by jungle and forest wherein elephants, leopards, and other wild animals roam, twelve or fifteen Britishers rule, with an authority never challenged, more than forty thousand adventurous Asiatics—men whose vocation is largely based on their daring, and whose competing religions and castes possess the germ of fanaticism that might be roused to bloodshed. The white man's control is supported by the presence of two hundred policemen, it is true, but these are natives. The keynote of this exposition of a multitude ruled by a handful of Europeans is the absolute fairness of their control, of course. Were justice non-existent, it would be inviting disaster for the white official to apprehend a wrong-doer, place him on trial, and personally administer with lash or birch the corporal punishment to be witnessed any morning in front of the camp lockup.

And what might happen if the divers, through their ringleaders, objected to surrendering to the Ceylon government the demanded "rake-off" of two thirds the oysters rescued from the sea by their efforts, in the event of these courageous fellows being assured that all the law in the world on the subject says that all the sea and all therein contained, beyond the distance of three nautical miles from shore, belongs to the universe? But the Manar diver knows naught of the three-mile law, presumably.

Does the fishery pay? Tremendously, so far as facts upon which to base an answer are obtainable. The government treasury is sometimes enormously expanded as a result of the enterprise. In 1905, the most prosperous of all Manar fisheries, the government sold its fifty million oysters for two and one half million rupees, and at least $600,000 of this was profit. Years ago, it is true, there were several fisheries producing for the treasury nothing but deficits. Nobody ever knows what reward visits the purchasers of oysters, for it is their habit to spread the report of non-success and disappointment. But the buyers and speculators come each year in larger numbers, with augmented credits, and they pay in competition with their kind a larger price for the oysters. The conclusion is, therefore, that they find the business profitable.

Even rumors of luck and profit would bring more speculators and rising prices at the auction sales, manifestly. Reports of fortunate strikes at Marichchikkaddi may more frequently be heard in India than in Ceylon, let it be said; and it is the gilded grandees of Hind—princes, maharajahs and rajahs—rather than the queens of Western society, who become possessors of the trove of Manar.

No Colombo merchant or magnate, or man or woman of the official set, is superior to tempting fortune by buying a few thousand oysters freshly landed from Marichchikkaddi. And the interminable question of caste, banning many things to Cingalese and Tamil, inhibits not the right to gamble upon the contents of a sackful of bivalves. If the fishery be successful, all Ceylon teems with stories of lucky finds, and habitations ranging from the roadside hut to the aristocratic bungalow in the Cinnamon Gardens are pointed to as having been gained by a productive deal in oysters. A favorite tale is that of the poor horse-tender, who, buying a few cents' worth of oysters, found the record pearl of the year; another is of the 'rickshawman suspected of having money in the bank as a result of a lucky find on the sea-front of Colombo of three or four oysters dropped from a discharging boat—in a shaded alley between buildings he forced the bivalves to disgorge a pearl worth hundreds of pounds sterling. Most stories of this character are as untrue as the reports of soubrettes and telephone boys winning fortunes in Wall Street.

Did I try my luck? Of course I did. Who could resist the temptation? I purchased two great sackfuls of oysters, a thousand in number, which were brought off to the government tug *Active* by salaaming peons from the government agent's office. At five o'clock the tug was ready to start Colomboward the instant the "despatches" I was to deliver came on board. At last the precious package, with a parade of red tape and impressive wax seals, was handed over the side. It may have contained something as priceless as a last year's directory; I never knew. It was my deep-seated suspicion, however, that the packet was somebody's excuse for letting the public treasury expend a few hundred rupees in carrying one in private life back to Colombo to catch his steamer for China the next evening.

Confident was I that the bags on the stern grating that had been freshly soused with seawater as the *Active* steamed away from Marichchikkaddi contained a wealth of pearls. In the cool of the early morning I would subsidize the eight native sailors, getting them to open the shelled treasures, while I garnered the pearls. With this thought uppermost, I turned in on a cushionless bench to snatch a few hours' sleep. But slumber was out of the question; my brain was planning what might be done with the pearls I was soon to possess. Yes, there surely would be plenty for a pearl-studded tiara for the loved one awaiting me; and any superfluity might be made into ropes and collars for admiring relatives at home. Cousin Jessie had always coveted a necklace of pearls with a diamond clasp. The dainty baubles were in those sacks; there was no question about that. Yes, my luck at pearl-getting would compensate for missing Sir Thomas Lipton's dinner in Colombo. Sleep always comes in time, and at last I was dreaming of the cargo of priceless gems with me on the boat.

How extremely uncomfortable the bench was! What was that? I was not asleep, but very wide-awake—and such pains! In an instant I was rolling on the deck and shrieking from the terribleness of my suffering. Could it be cholera, the plague, or simply appendicitis with which I was stricken? The sailors held me down, but not a soul on board knew a word of English. I was positive that my end had come, and the thought of expiring away from friends and with a pocketful of prepaid around-the-world tickets was not agreeable. In an hour the pain was excruciating, and it continued for ten long hours with varying severity. Morning came, and the Indian skipper was plying his furnace with lubricating oil and turpentine—with anything that would help him get me to Colombo and medical skill. At last, eighteen hours out from Marichchikkaddi, the *Active* was in the harbor and I was being carried to the Grand Oriental Hotel.

"What about the two bags of oysters, the

captain wishes to know?" the hotel interpreter asked.

"Oh, give them to the men," was the answer; "I have ceased to care for pearl-studded tiaras and collars. I 'm glad to get away alive from the decaying millions of oysters at the fishery. Even God's free air there is poisoned by them. What I want most is a doctor."

CHAPTER IV

UPWARD TO THE SHRINE OF BUDDHA

FROM Colombo it is but seventy-five miles to Ceylon's ancient capital, and the journey thither is picturesque almost beyond description. For fifty miles the railway leads through the rich vegetation of the lowlands, with groves of cocoanut palms seemingly as boundless as the sea. In a suburb of Colombo the sacred Kelani River is crossed, at a point not remote from the Buddhist temple claimed to be contemporary with Gautama himself. The valley of the Kelani is vivid with rice-fields of green. The line then pushes its way through a bewildering medley of tropical vegetation—there are miles of cashew and breadfruit trees, of frangipani and jaks, and more than once a stately talipot-palm is discerned in full blossom—for half a century the tree has stored its vitality for this one effort; and the burst of splendor spent, its career on earth is ended. For twenty-five miles the train zigzags up hills, running now and then on the edge of a shelf from whence the traveler looks down hundreds of feet sheer upon foam-crested rapids. The journey from Colombo

A LADY OF KANDY

to Kandy affords one of the memorable experiences of Ceylon.

England has held the interior region of the island, controlled for centuries by the Kandyan kings, for but ninety odd years, and it is curious to observe wings of palaces at Kandy, where a semi-barbaric rule long held sway, employed now as British administrative offices. Little antiquity is discernible in the old hill capital, due to former rival interests of the Portuguese and Dutch. When one nation had control of the picturesque town, it was customary to efface or demolish everything that the other had done.

Kandy is the city of Buddha's tooth, and as such is the object of unbounded reverence with more than four hundred million inhabitants of the earth. Oudh, where Gautama Buddha died, lacks the sacred importance of Kandy; and the sepulcher at Jerusalem means no more to Christians, nor Mecca and Medina to followers of Mahomet.

Kandy was but a mountain village when the holy molar was brought here in the sixteenth century for safe-keeping. The small temple wherein it was deposited was beautified and enlarged, and finally the priesthood made the place their principal seat, and the Kandyan kings later made the city their stronghold and capital of the country.

Thousands of pilgrims come yearly to offer to the Temple of the Tooth their gifts of gold and silver ornaments, coins, jewels, vestments for the priests, even fruits and flowers—and these devotees have traveled from every hamlet of Ceylon and from every land where Buddha has believers —from Nepaul, the Malay Peninsula, China, Japan, even from Siberia and Swedish Lapland. The kings of Burmah and Siam, in compliance with the wish of their subjects, send annual contributions toward the support of the temple enshrining the tooth; and Buddhist priests in far-away Japan correspond with the hierarchy of the temple of Kandy. No other tooth has the drawing power of this one, certainly.

Strange to say, Buddhism has been cast out from India, where it originated, by the Hindu faith, which it was meant to reform. In India's enormous population scarce seven millions to-day worship at Buddha's shrine. Christianity, as well, is a stranger to the land where it was born. It appears the irony of fate that these great religions, glorious in principle, have abiding places without number, save in the countries where they originated. But such is the fact.

Few scholars can study the tenets of Buddhism without the conviction that it is a religion of striking merit—that is, as form and dogma are described by writers and commentators; but as practised by races not far removed from pagan illiteracy, with whom idolatry and superstition are inherent, it may no longer be the perfection of doctrine that was espoused by Prince Gautama.

Sir Edwin Arnold, who thoroughly knew most Eastern religions, admired enthusiastically the precepts of Buddha, and no one can read his writings without experiencing some regard for the

Buddhism of literature. In "The Light of Asia" the five commandments of the great religion of the Orient are thus poetically recited:

> Kill not—for Pity's sake—and lest ye slay
> The meanest thing upon its upward way.
>
> Give freely and receive, but take from none
> By greed, or force or fraud, what is his own.
>
> Bear not false witness, slander not, nor lie;
> Truth is the speech of inward purity.
>
> Shun drugs and drinks which work the wit abuse;
> Clear minds, clean bodies, need no Soma juice.
>
> Touch not thy neighbor's wife, neither commit
> Sins of the flesh unlawful and unfit.

Whether present-day Buddhism is the exact religion taught by the princely priest, and gracefully described by the English poet, matters little —its fountainhead is Kandy, and temple and dependencies of the sacred bone form the Vatican of the faith. This miraculous tooth, alleged to be the left eye-tooth of Gautama Buddha, and taken from the ashes of his funeral pyre twenty-five hundred years ago, has played a mighty part in Eastern intrigue, and wars between nations have been fought over it. For centuries it was the priceless marriage dower going with certain favored princesses of royal blood. It was brought from India to Ceylon in the fourth century after

Christ. The Malabars secured it by conquest more than once, the Portuguese had it for a time at Goa, and for safety it was brought to Kandy in the sixteenth century, and it has there since been cared for with scrupulous fidelity.

A relic supported by so much history should at least be genuine—the history may be all right, but the tooth is a shambling hoax, at best a crude proxy for the molar of Gautama. Intelligent priests of Buddhism must know this, but the millions of common people finding solace in the faith have never heard the truth—and would n't believe it if they did. No more amazing display of faith over a reputed sacred relic is known than is associated with this bogus tooth of Kandy.

Reference to any library of unimpeachable works on the world's religions proves conclusively that the actual tooth was burned by the Catholic archbishop of Goa in 1560, in the presence of the viceroy of India and his suite—this is authentic history. Six years after the event at Goa a spurious tooth had to be provided to effect an international marriage long under contract, and the molar of a wild boar or of an ape was used. This tooth eventually was brought to the town nestling in the hills of Ceylon, and surrounding it grew the capital of the proud kingdom of the Kandyans. In the year of Waterloo, the British overthrew the reigning sovereign, and the bogus tooth and its temple have since had the protection of English rule.

The dimensions of the tooth are fatal to its pre-

TEMPLE OF THE TOOTH, KANDY

tended genuineness, for it is a discolored ivory two inches in length and one in diameter. No human mouth ever gave shelter to such a tooth. To view it would be a test of credulity too trying even for fanaticism to stand. The hoax, consequently, is concealed from sight. On important occasions it is displayed—at a distance. When the Duke and Duchess of York visited Kandy the high priests of the temple exhibited the tooth; and on occasions it is supposed to be carried in processions through the streets on the back of an elephant—but deception and trickery in connection with the tooth come easy.

The enshrined humbug reposes on a massive silver table, encrusted with gems and festooned with jeweled chains. The chamber in which it is kept in the temple is stiflingly hot, with atmosphere heavy from the perfume of flowers. Within six or eight bell-shaped metal covers the tooth is held by a standard as if emerging from the petals of a lotus flower of gold. Visitors to the museum at Colombo may see a replica of the relic and its setting: it is a tawdry, unimpressive object.

Glance where you will in Kandy, drive in any direction, penetrate any avenue or footpath, and priestly disciples of Buddha, of every age from the novice to the patriarch of exalted rank, accost the vision. Pilgrims appear to be constantly arriving. They are present from Jaffna in the north, from Galle in the south, from Nuara Eliya in the mountains, from everywhere—some come on foot, some by curious carts drawn by buffaloes or bullocks, some by railroad train. All are unshod, and the head of each is bare and shaven. Each wears the robe of eternal yellow, with an arm and shoulder bare, and the sunshade and palm fan have been the adjuncts of the brotherhood since Gautama left his royal parents' house to teach the word of Buddha.

Celibacy is the rule of the priesthood. Nothing can be less obtrusive than the demeanor of the brethren. Visitors to their temples are welcomed, and courteous replies are always made to inquiries.

Cremation is general in the priesthood, but apparently optional with others of the faith. When a dignitary of the priesthood passes away his confrères assemble from far and near at the funeral pyre to do him honor. The incineration usually takes place in a palm grove. The corpse is surrounded with dried wood, made additionally inflammable with oils. The rites of the pyre include nothing of a sensational character; the assemblage chants for a time, then a priest of high rank applies the torch, and in an hour nothing remains but a mound of embers and ashes. A cremation may be readily witnessed at Kandy or Colombo, or other place possessing a considerable population.

The peoples of low caste of the East are too numerous to be catalogued. India teems with them, of course, and the paradise island of Ceylon has a considerable percentage of human beings denied by their betters of almost every privilege save breathing the free air of heaven. The lowlands and coastal regions have been so commercialized that human pariahs are there almost overlooked—but they are at every turning of the road in every hamlet, everywhere. Kandy, once royal city, knows the abhorred low caste to-day as it did five hundred years ago, for in plain view of the capital in the hills there are settlements of men and women still excluded from communion with the world by reason of a royal curse pronounced centuries ago—and it is a condition worse than death itself.

Representatives of the Rodiya caste may be seen any day by pedestrians in the city's outskirts. There are not many of them, fortunately—perhaps a thousand all told. Tradition has it that hundreds of years ago a vengeful monarch condemned their race to never-ending degradation for having supplied the royal table with human flesh instead of venison. Custom forces these poor mortals to ford or swim a stream, instead of using a ferry; and forbids their drawing water at public wells. They must not live in houses like other people, but in hovels constructed usually by leaning a hurdle against a rock, and their men and women must never clothe their bodies above the waist. Until recent years courts of justice have been closed to them, and if overtaken on their travels by darkness they must find shelter in caves or abandoned hovels. They recognize their degradation by falling on their knees when addressing even toilers on the highway, and shout a warning on the approach of a traveler, that he may halt long enough for them to get off the road to secure his passing without possibility of defilement.

These groveling worms of the earth are nominally Buddhists, but are forbidden to enter a temple. Hence they pray "standing afar off." Demon worship is accredited to them. Their headman can officiate only when he has obtained the sanction of the common jailor of the district. Even to ask alms they must not enter a fenced property, and it is said at Kandy that water over which their shadows have fallen is held to be so defiled that other natives will not use it until purified by the sun's rays. And thus it is; their race is penalized in every manner, and the ban goes unchallenged by the miserable beings.

Their denial by mankind of ordinary fellowship has driven them to filthy and beastly habits. They devour the flesh of monkeys and tortoises, even carrion, it is claimed; and of late years they haunt feasts and ceremonials hoping to obtain fragments of food thrown from the tables of their betters. Now and then they are paid something for watching fields, and for burying carcasses of dead cattle. It is not known that they are thieves, but they are shunned as if they were. In emergencies, when there is a scarcity of labor, they are induced to work on tea estates, or at road mending; but the habits of vagabondage are too rooted to allow their remaining long in useful employment.

Superior in every way to their men, the Rodiya women are the most beautiful in all Ceylon.

CREMATION OF A BUDDHIST PRIEST

Their scantiness of raiment, it is pleaded in their behalf, is due in no sense to immodesty. Rodiya girls wander the country as dancers and jugglers, and their erect figures, elastic step, and regalness of carriage, would be envied by the proudest woman promenading Vanity Fair; some of them have faces so perfect in a classic way that a sculptor or painter might make himself famous by reproducing them.

Believe not that these miserable people represent the lowest grade of degradation in Lanka's isle, for there are two outcast races so far beneath them in the social scale as to be avoided by Rodiyas as if they reeked with a pestilential disease. These castes are hopelessly beyond the pale.

British rule in Asia recognizes no caste distinctions, but it has been a humane work of the wives of several English governors of Ceylon to seek to improve the position of the women of the Rodiya caste, especially of the young girls. Some benefit is claimed as a result of the efforts of the English women—but the majesty and power of Great Britain are puny institutions compared with the force of caste among native races. To keep down the Rodiya population a certain Kandyan king, it is stated on good authority, used to have a goodly number of them shot each year.

CHAPTER V

IN CEYLON'S HILL COUNTRY

WHEN good Kandyans discourse in flowery vein, they say Kandy is only forty miles from heaven. Visitors who have fallen under the charm of the place are more likely to wonder at their moderation than question their ability to measure celestial distances. If Gautama Buddha's "eternal rest" were to be had on earth, Kandy would surely be the reward of Nirvana promised those who have acquired merit.

The beauty of Kandy is based upon naturalness; it is not grand like Taormina in Sicily, nor produced by nature and art in combination like Monte Carlo. Everything connected with the spot is fascinating, even the jungle that by day harbors the jackals which sometimes make night hideous to sojourners. Everybody appears happy; even elephants hauling timber in the suburbs toil cheerfully.

This inland province that formed the kingdom of Kandy preserved its integrity throughout the Portuguese and Dutch invasions of the island; and the English were in possession of the coast section full nineteen years before the Kandyan monarchy succumbed to their power.

This beautiful city was a different place under the native kings. They loved grandeur, apparently, but it was the grandeur of selfish surroundings and luxury. The lake now the center of the city was constructed by the last king, it is true; but its shore witnessed atrocities never surpassed in savage excess. Near the spot where stands a monastery of yellow robed monks of Buddha, the last king assembled his people in 1814 to witness the punishment of the innocent wife and children of a fleeing official accused of treason. By the blow of a sword the head of each child was severed from its body in the mother's presence, even that of the babe wrenched from her breast. The heads were placed in a mortar, and the woman forced under threat of disgraceful torture to pound them with a huge pestle.

When news of this reached the coast the English determined to intervene in the interests of humanity. While the horror was yet fresh in the public mind, a party of native merchants of Colombo came to Kandy to trade. The fiendish king ordered them seized and horribly mutilated. When, a few weeks later, the survivors returned to the sea-coast deprived of ears, noses and hands—with the severed members tied to their necks—the English decided to act immediately. Three months later Kandy was in their possession, and the king an exile in southern India.

From that time, with the exception of a few years when the hereditary Kandyan chiefs were troublesome through finding their privileges circumscribed, the progress of Ceylon as a whole has been remarkable. Perhaps the finest example of benefits coming with England's colonial rule is this "Eden of the Eastern Wave." Slavery and forced labor on public works have been abolished, fine roads constructed everywhere, and adequate educational facilities placed within easy reach.

A visitor perceives no squalor, few beggars, and apparently no genuine poverty. All these advantages have been secured practically without taxing the natives in any manner. Uniform contentment, consequently, is everywhere visible. The naked babies, looking like india-rubber dolls, have apparently never learned to cry.

Oddly enough, the English made Kandy the Saint Helena of Arabi Pasha's exile, until the broken and aged man was permitted a few years since to return to his beloved Egypt.

Itself beautiful with poinsettia, bougainvillea, crotons, hibiscus and palms, a botanical garden in Kandy would seem to have no proper place. But the city possesses one that is almost unique among tropical gardens. It is in the suburb of Peradeniya, four miles out, and it is embraced on three sides by Ceylon's principal stream, the Mahavali-ganga. For eighty years the Ceylon government has treated the Peradeniya garden and its associated experimental stations as an investment—and it has paid well, for through its agency the cultivation of cinchona, cacao, rubber and other economic crops has been introduced to the people.

SCREW PINE

ASSAM RUBBER TREE

TREES IN PERADENIYA GARDEN, KANDY

Throughout Asia the Peradeniya garden is famous. Whether the claim that it is the finest in the world be correct would require an expert to determine. The botanical garden at Demerara may be as good, if not larger and better.

A layman visiting Peradeniya returns to Kandy in a state of bewilderment. He has seen so many attractive and strange manifestations of nature that lucid description is beyond his power. He is aware, nevertheless, that he has viewed nearly every tree, shrub, plant and vine known to tropical and subtropical climes; shrubs that produce every spice, perfume and flavoring he ever heard of, or that contribute to medicine, as well.

At Peradeniya the palm family has nearly a hundred representatives, including the areca, palmyra, talipot, royal, fan, traveler's, date and cocoanut. The forty or more varieties of crotons include the curious corkscrew of the West Indies, and range extravagantly in colors and markings. Huge Assam rubber-trees have exposed roots suggesting a tangle of octopi. A tree noticeable for its perfect foliage is the breadfruit; and there are sensitive plants that shrink from intimate attention, and water-plants whose roots need not come into contact with the earth.

Here and there are kola trees, cardamom bushes, aloe plants from which sisal is drawn, camphor and cinnamon shrubs, and probably every species of the parasitical family, depending like many human beings upon stronger relatives or neighbors for support. The orchid enclosure would arouse any collector's covetousness. There are foliage plants producing leaves counterfeiting elephant ears, and others that look like full spread peacock tails. A small leaf which the official guide of the gardens is obviously partial to is deep green when held to the light, purple when slightly turned, and deep red if looked at from another angle. The visitor moves swiftly into the sunlight when told that he is standing in the shade of the deadly upas.

A traveler approaching the island of Ceylon hears constantly of the wonders of Peradeniya; and some statements in praise of the garden are taken usually with reserve, especially that asserting there are trees there which develop so rapidly that the spectator can actually see them grow. This seems incredible, but there is ample basis for the statement. After a rain the fronds of the giant bamboo frequently grow a foot in the course of a day. At the office of the director of the garden are records of many measurements proving that fronds have lengthened a half inch in an hour. A tree growing a half inch in sixty minutes is a Ceylon fact. The first time I went to Peradeniya, thousands of flying-foxes, suspended bat-like from the giant bamboos a hundred feet from the earth, were sleeping away the day, while soaring above the trees were hundreds of these queer objects, scolding like disturbed crows.

Peradeniya's visitors come from every land in the world, some traveling great distances to see the wonders of the garden. One has not to be ar-

TAMIL COOLIE SETTING OUT TEA PLANTS

boriculturist or botanist to appreciate the establishment; it is always entertaining, sometimes amusing, and appeals variously to the tastes of visitors. For example, the Mexican goes involuntarily to the aloe from which his beloved pulque is made, the Egyptian to the date-palm, the Connecticut man to the nutmeg grove, and the New Yorker to the tree under which handfuls of cloves may be scooped up without charge, whereas at home they are acquired one at a time at considerable expense.

Explore the highways and byways of Kandy keenly as one may, nothing is in evidence explaining its manifest prosperity—the place has no distinctive product or business. It is the seat of management, however, of the island's greatest industry—tea raising.

In Ceylon tea is "king." This being the fact, no visitor to the town where the Planters' Association has its administrative machinery can close his ears to tea talk. Elsewhere people talk over their tea-cups; in Kandy, they talk tea over every other kind of cup. Kandy's big hotel bristles with planters in overspreading sun hats, as do club and friendly bungalow verandas. Some are "down" for a day (and a night) from up-country estates, while others are "up" from smallish properties at levels below Kandy. Nearly all have to purchase supplies and draw a few sacks of rupees from the bank with which to pay off their coolies. But some have come to discuss market conditions and prospects with their agents. A few, not yet wholly emancipated from the social side of life in which they were reared, have journeyed to Kandy to rub shoulders for a few days with civilization.

The orbit of each and every one of these transplanted Britons is tea, and this in its primal form. They can have no concern with Steel common, Amalgamated copper or Erie 4's, and to them the jargon of stock exchanges would be as meaningless as Sanskrit platitudes. Their speculative medium is tea—tea in bulk, and pretty large bulk at that.

The daily cable from London summarizing the tea market interests each of these men as vitally as the tale of the ticker interests the American taking a flier in stocks. The story is told in two or three lines, and by a presentation of numerals appearing exceedingly unimportant to the sojourner whose operations in tea never exceeded the purchase of a pound package.

Yes, the figures tell the story—a tale of occasional success, but often of failure and woe. A bracketed set of fractions explains the range of prices for broken pekoes, another set deals with common pekoes, another with orange pekoes, and still another with common souchongs. Then follow such words as "steady," "generally firm," and "somewhat lower"—each a phrase with potential significance. The crux of the communication, like that of a school-girl's letter, comes last. If it reads "general market closed 1-8th penny up," the planter has visions of happiness and affluence, and forthwith orders a "peg." But

TAMIL GIRL PLUCKING TEA

if the postscript says "1-8th down," the young planter foresees nothing but disaster, and may consider levanting with the bags of rupees by the next steamer from Colombo. A planter is always a bull on prices, while the important buyer in Europe is chronically bearish.

The yearly tea product of Ceylon is aggregating 155,000,000 pounds, and of this Uncle Sam purchases 12,000,000 pounds, while 98,000,000 go to Great Britain. The value of the annual output varies little from $21,000,000—and from this Ceylon supports itself so comfortably that the tea-plant seems to merit adoption as the emblem of the colony.

The rise of the industry affords one of the most remarkable instances of rapid development of an agricultural pursuit. Coffee used to be the dominating crop in the island, until "coffee blight" ruined the industry. Tea was then experimented with. In 1875 barely a thousand acres were under tea; now the acreage is 385,000. A journey from Kandy to Nuwara Eliya, in the mountains, is through an interminable tea-garden, and on every hand is proof of substantial investment of capital. The choicest crops are raised between five and six thousand feet above sea-level, and lands in this zone are worth as much as $500 an acre. The scientific cultivation of tea paid its pioneers handsomely, but the current opinion is that overproduction is killing prices, and that a new crop must be sought—probably rubber.

Ceylon's important tea estates are the property

of companies, whose shares are dealt in on the London and Colombo stock exchanges. Small plantations are owned by individuals, usually the persons conducting them. One or two thousand Europeans, mainly Englishmen and Scotchmen, are employed on the important estates as managers, assistants and accountants. Hosts of young Britons work a year or two without compensation for the experience. They are called "creepers," and some of them eventually obtain salaried offices, or embark in the industry on their own account. The laboring force on an estate is provided chiefly by Tamil coolies from southern India, and numbers from one to two thousand. Both men and women contrive to lay by a competence at a wage rate of from eight to fifteen cents a day.

If let alone, the tea-plant would grow to be a tree eighteen or twenty feet high, but by generous top pruning it is kept down to three feet, thus becoming a squat bush possessing a biggish leafing area. Every eight or twelve days the shoots and young leaves are plucked—when treated these become the tea of commerce. Tea-plants are alike, speaking generally, grades being effected by the discrimination of picker and sorter. Fresh buds and tender young leaves make the pekoes, older ones the souchongs. Tea gathered exclusively from buds and tips is called "flowery;" if the first young leaf be included, it is "orange pekoe." In order of quality the Ceylon grades are: orange pekoe, pekoe, pekoe-souchong, souchong, congou, and dust.

A KANDYAN CHIEFTAIN

Tea-plants are perennial, and are set about four feet apart on hillsides. At three years of age they become productive. Familiar sights in the hills are the coolies with baskets of slips setting out plants wherever unemployed spaces may be found, and groups of Tamil girls plucking buds and young leaves from mature bushes. These girls are happy countenanced, some slender and graceful in carriage and movement, and none express objection to being snapshotted by travelers. The girls' baskets are emptied and contents systematically sorted at convenient places in the field, or at the factory. Essential to every important estate is the factory, for there the leaves are withered, broken by rolling, fermented, fired, and finally sifted into grades preparatory to packing in lead-lined boxes ready to be despatched to the markets of the universe.

It is reassuring to witness the system and scrupulous cleanliness of every step employed in producing Ceylon tea. Anybody who has spent a day on an up-country estate is fairly certain to be friendly to Ceylon tea the rest of his life, for modern machinery does much of the work which in China and Japan is performed by hands none too clean and amid surroundings none too healthful.

CHAPTER VI

BOMBAY AND ITS PARSEE "JEES" AND "BHOYS"

THE Parsee is the only sect holding religious tenets strange enough to stamp them as "peculiar people" who amount to much in the material affairs of life. Every country possesses groups of people having religious beliefs and practices which attract to them a curious interest; but Bombay's Parsee colony is the only illustration of a brotherhood following strange lives who shine resplendently in the financial and social worlds.

Everything in Bombay is dominated by the Parsee element, and every public hospital and other charitable institution, public statue, or drinking fountain, is the benefaction of a Parsee. The mansions and finest villas are Parsee homes, the leaders of club life are Parsees, and almost every bank and influential commercial house bears a Parsee name on its door. Bombay's population is not far from nine hundred thousand, of which the Parsees number only sixty thousand—but this minority impresses its importance on the majority and gives a character of unique interest to the city.

These dominating people are Indians only by

adoption. Twelve hundred years ago the Mohammedan conquerors of Persia persecuted the disciples of Zoroaster to an extent that many of the strongest men and women of the faith fled to India for safety, and the Parsees of to-day are the descendants of these refugees. For generations they have made education a feature, have always helped each other, and been extremely clannish, although preserving toward people of other religions a respectful attitude. Their creed, claimed to have descended from the Hebrew prophet Daniel, is expressed in three precepts of two words each: Good thoughts, good words, good deeds. Orthodox Parsees wear a white girdle of three coils as reminder of these principles; but present-day Parsee men have discarded all evidences of their creed save the designating vizorless cap, and dress in garments of European pattern, and their women are garbed in robes of delicately-shaded and clinging silks, and wear embroidered mantillas on their heads.

Most Parsees are superbly educated, variously accomplished, and speak English fluently. Their equipages are the smartest in Bombay, and every walk of life is led by them. The great fortunes of this part of India are theirs, and Parsee names are identified with everything contributing to Bombay's importance. These names are strikingly peculiar, are usually of from four to six syllables, the last being usually "jee" or "bhoy." The Jeejeebhoy family is intensely Parsee, of course, and important enough to possess an English baronetcy. The city's principal hospital was the gift of Jamsetjee Jeejeebhoy. Other families of renown in the financial world are the Readymoneys, Jehangirs and Sassoons.

Turn where you may the eye meets something donated to the public by generous Parsees. These people have long been loyal supporters of British rule in India, and frequently able to neutralize Hindu or Mohammedan opposition to a public measure. Baronetcies and knighthoods have consequently been showered upon them from London. Incidentally, a good deal of the money with which hospitals and libraries were given by great Parsees of a former generation came as reward for running a successful "corner" in Indian cotton at the time of America's civil war. Lancashire mills could get no staple from the Southern states, and astute Bombay capitalists, securing control of the native crop, held the same until the price advanced from ten or twelve cents to a dollar a pound. The fruits of this *coup*, some of them at least, dotted Bombay with noble buildings and statues.

Some Parsees drive public street vehicles, work on tramways and railways, and pursue humbler vocations, it is true; but most Parsees dwell in princely homes and go to their offices and clubs in splendidly appointed broughams and victorias. Success in life even in Parseedom is based upon the principle of survival of the fittest—or astutest.

The Parsees stoutly deny that they are fire worshippers. The sacred flame perpetually burning

PARSEE TOWER OF SILENCE, BOMBAY

in their houses of worship, brought by their ancestors from Persia, is but a symbol, they insist. God, according to their faith, is the emblem of glory, refulgence, and spiritual life; therefore they face the holy flame when praying as the most fitting symbol of the Deity. In the open air they prostrate themselves when praying to the setting sun. Parsee temples are plain to severity, with walls bare and floors uncovered and empty; but there is always the recess wherein burns the sacred fire of incense and sandalwood.

The method of dealing with the Parsee dead is startlingly original, and said to be in strict keeping with the teaching of Zoroaster. According to Parsee tenets fire is too highly venerated to be polluted by burning the dead, while water is equally respected, and Mother Earth as well. Hence the Parsees offer their dead to the elements and the birds of the air, and the bones of rich and poor, high and low, even of the malefactor and suicide, are consigned to eternity in crumbled state in a common pit.

The Towers of Silence occupy the finest site on Malabar Hill, overlooking beautiful Bombay, and high above the Arabian Sea—it is Nature's beauty spot, embowered in graceful shrubbery and palms, with fragrant flowers everywhere. The governor of Bombay Presidency resides at Malabar Point, further along, and the homes of men high in officialdom or commerce occupy every available site in the neighborhood. The Towers, five in number, are of whitewashed stone and cement, 275 feet in circumference, and perhaps twenty-five feet high. An iron door admits the corpse of the Parsee, and once within the strange building it is proffered to the birds of the air—gloating vultures, coarse and repugnant in every aspect.

Four carriers of the dead are seen approaching the beautiful garden with a bier on their shoulders. Two bearded men, the only living persons permitted to enter a Tower, come next. Then follow from fifty to a hundred mourners and friends in pure white robes, walking two and two, each couple holding a handkerchief between them in token of a united grief. The apex of the hill reached, the mourners turn into the house of prayer, wherein the eternal fire is burning, or take position beneath spreading palms for solitary meditation. The bearers deliver the corpse to the bearded functionaries at the entrance to the Tower, and these carry it within. The floor of the Tower is of iron grating with three circles whereon the corpses are placed. The inner circle is for children, the next for women, and the outer for men.

The bearded men are lost to view for a minute or two only, and their concluding office within is to remove the shroud, leaving the body wholly bare. The iron door clangs as they emerge, there is a mighty whir of wings, and in a twinkling the corpse is in possession of hundreds of greedy, competing vultures. In twenty minutes not a vestige of flesh remains on the bones, and the loathsome birds resume their watch from the edge of the Tower for the next comer. Their experienced gaze perceives a funeral procession a mile away in the direction of the city, and a signal cry is so readily understood by vultures resting on trees in the neighborhood that a unanimous attendance is assured long before the corpse passes the portal of the grounds.

The human skeletons are left within the Tower to disintegrate by action of sun and wind, heat and cold. In time the bearded men, gloved and with tongs, remove them to a vast well in the middle of the enclosure, where with lapse of time they turn to dust.

Corpses being considered unclean by Parsee standards, carriers of the dead, as well as those who enter the Towers, are assigned to a class by themselves, and forbidden to mix with others of their strange religion. There is a superstition that an awful curse would be visited upon an unauthorized person whose gaze fell upon a body or skeleton inside a Tower of Silence. The habiliments of those whose duty takes them within are always destroyed before they leave the grounds.

Whatever may be claimed in defense of the Parsee method of dealing with their dead, from a sanitary standpoint, the custom possesses an aspect gruesome in the extreme. The Hindus' system of burning on the river bank is even less repulsive.

If any city in the East is sport-mad it is Bombay. Men work there mornings and engage in something of a sportive character afternoons. The school-boy, even, slings his books from a hockey stick, and the departmental clerk sets out for an afternoon's sociability accompanied by his faithful tennis racquet. Nowhere can better polo be seen than on the Marine Lines Maidan; as for cricket, there probably are more players in Bombay, British and native, than in any town of its population in England—and Bombay's cricket is of the best. More than once have crack teams out from England been heartlessly beaten by local Parsee players. Golf is considered too slow. The next best thing to being a member of the nobility is for a Briton to belong to the Royal Bombay Yacht Club, for it gives him the *cachet* to everything Asiatic. The club-house on the Apollo Bunder possesses the best situation on the water front, and from its verandas fashionables watch matches that are sailed with consummate skill. During winter months foot-ball appeals strongly to the soldier class, while motor-car races and trials appear to be daily events.

It is the horse that is king, however, in Bombay's pastimes. The Hunt Club sends the smart set to the suburbs now and then, and tent-pegging and pig-sticking draw biggish audiences from the military class whenever contests are announced. But the paramount sport of the masses is horse-racing, pure and simple. The course is on the plains a few miles out of town, close to a suburb given over to cotton-mills, where nearly as many spindles fly as at Fall River. All Bombay seems to be at the races, irrespective of religious or social distinctions—everyone present loves the

A BOMBAY RAILWAY STATION

horse and appears possessed of a goodly supply of rupees with which to back his selections.

The Jockey Club has its own lawn and private enclosure on the stand, and there is a box for the governor and anybody coming from Government House. The grand-stand bears a minor importance to the betting ring, for the latter holds a surging, throbbing medley of humanity—society folk from India's innermost official set, sleek Parsees wearing gold rimmed eye-glasses, rajahs from all parts, wealthy merchants and bankers, fez-wearing Mohammedans from the world of Islam, men from the Persian Gulf in astrachan head-gear, Pathans from beyond the Himalayas, Sikhs from the Punjab—as can be gathered in great India, the museum of the human race.

Three score book-makers howl their bargains in raucous tones, and a whirlwind of rupee paper passes to the strong boxes. The crowd is backing the favorites. Even the Arab horse dealers from the Bhendi bazaar, manly fellows in the garb of desert sheikhs, whose pockets bulge with rolls of notes, comprehend the book-makers' jargon of English that might be incomprehensible to an Oxford don. A prince who is heir to the rulership of one of the greatest states in India has no scruples against inviting an expression of opinion as to so-and-so's bay filly of a native sportsman with beard dyed red with henna, in keeping with the fashion of his kind. Escorted ladies of position, and unescorted women in pairs from Grant Road, are present before the betting booths.

Fair Parsee ladies, wearing clinging robes of delicate shades, wait patiently while their swains place their money on the impending event.

A bell rings loudly—the horses are at the post. The mob rushes from the betting ring to the lawn; only few take the trouble to climb to their seats. It is a quick race. The crowd of standees in the inner field see it best, and down this mighty nondescript body is echoed the cry "Kedge Anchor!" Sure enough, "Kedge Anchor," an unknown from Australia, ridden by a jockey of obscure past, wins the great race. Three favorites are ingloriously beaten. Up go the numbers. All is over in less than two minutes—and the crowd goes pell-mell back to the book-makers' enclosure, hoping for better luck over the next race on the card. If rupees were dollars, the financial aspect of a Bombay racing day would be important.

Kipling wrote true when he called Bombay "India's Queen City." It lacks the depressing influences of Calcutta, as well as the odors. Indeed, it is one of the handsomest cities of the whole British Empire, and has more notable buildings than Manchester or Edinburgh. True, its stately piles blend the Gothic and Indian schools of architecture, but otherwise there is nothing Eastern about Bombay—save its people. A man awakening from long slumber on a ship anchored off the Apollo Bunder would willingly swear he beheld a European town. Eight tenths of India's visitors arrive and depart from Bombay.

The opening of the Suez Canal made certain the

importance of Bombay as a trade center. It is now the largest cotton port in the world next to New Orleans, and if plague and smallpox might be controlled for five years it would have a population of a million. Bombay is a comparatively modern city, as cities count in immemorial India. England secured Bombay in 1661, not by conquest, but as a portion of the marriage dowry of Catharine of Braganza of Portugal, when she became the queen of Charles II.

The world's most artistic railway station—not the largest, nor costliest—is in Bombay, and the best marble statue in existence of Queen Victoria was presented to the Bombay municipality by His Highness the Gaekwar of Baroda. Another notable gift is the bronze statue of Edward VII, donated by Sir Albert Sassoon, son of a public-spirited banker from Baghdad, who took up his residence in Bombay. A newcomer among the city's office buildings is "Roosevelt House," advantageously situated near the Apollo Bunder.

The eyes of the person recently arrived from Europe or America behold many strange and amusing sights in the streets of Bombay, and for days your local guide and the obliging porter at the hotel is kept busy the livelong day answering questions. The native policeman is a human institution who explains himself. It is averred that he is loyal and efficient, but with his calfless legs bared to the knee and feet shod in sandals, he looks a queer cousin of Fifth Avenue's "Finest" and of the "Bobby" of London. A person unaccustomed to the habits of subject races gets the idea that the Bombay constable's first duty is the touching of his cap to white men, all and sundry; but it is said to his credit that in a street brawl or a water front quarrel among drunken lascars he fights like a wildcat. He is extremely proud of his truncheon, for it is a badge of office tremendously respected in the city's labyrinths where India's heterogeneous peoples dwell a dozen or more in a room. During the wet monsoon the policeman of Bombay carries an umbrella supplied by the municipality, which heightens his comical aspect—but it keeps him dry.

The markings and badges of caste observed in Bombay streets lead you to a constant interrogation of your sources of information. At the outset you determine to obtain an understanding of the institution of Indian caste, but a fortnight after your arrival in Bombay you conclude that the task is too great for anybody having other things to do, and give it up in despair. A few facts connected with this supreme and dominating characteristic take root in your memory, however, and you have learned that the customs and rites of caste could not be strengthened even by legal enactments, or by the massed strength of all the armies on earth. The word is derived from the Latin word *castus,* implying purity of blood, and whose essential principle is marriage. India's population groups forty-seven nationalities, divided into 2,378 recognized castes and tribes. Accident of birth determines irrevocably a native's so-

BOMBAY POLICEMAN

cial and domestic relationship, prescribing even what he may eat and drink throughout life, how he must dress, and whom he may marry. There are four fundamental divisions of caste—the priestly or Brahmin (which has close upon fifteen million devotees), the warrior, the trading, and the laboring; and these have interminable subdivisions. Below the laboring caste there is a substratum which is termed pariah or outcast, and these degraded specimens of humanity are not better than animated machines performing the functions of public scavengers.

Throughout India caste is hereditary. The son of a priest becomes a priest, a warrior's son becomes a soldier, and a carpenter's boy a carpenter, and so on. For a father to start a son in any calling but his own, or a vocation that is similar, would be "against his caste." Caste is social as well as religious, and includes the occupation as well as the creed. For a Hindu to rise from his inherited caste is next to impossible, and this tends to make the Hindus an ambitionless race. The infusion of new blood is likewise not tolerated, and in India "caste" and "custom" are perfect synonyms—and each a national curse.

A major part of the people of India are agriculturists, men and women who are dependent upon what they can wrest from the soil for their existence. Their plough, an heirloom from remote antiquity, merely scratches the earth. The use of superior implements would result in superior tillage and augmented crops; but it would be as simple to induce the peasant to change his religion as to get him to forsake the plough used by his ancestors. The implements of daily life mostly belong to the barbarous ages. Attempt to introduce any other and you are rebuked by the reply: "It is not the custom; my father used this article, and therefore it is my duty to use it. Would you have me set myself up for a wiser person than my revered parent?" The toiling masses, consequently, are poor—and seem destined to remain poor until the close of the chapter.

I heard of a contractor engaged in building a railway who objected to the physical toil and slowness of having a bank of earth removed by baskets on the heads of coolies. So he invested in a number of wheelbarrows and explained their use to the natives, and went back to his Bombay office flattering himself that he was a reformer. The next week when he visited the scene of operations he found the barrows in use, but the coolies were filling them with dirt and carrying them up the bank on their heads as they had always carried their baskets. The coolie of Hind is not to be beguiled by any demonstration intended to lighten his task, for he is crusted with conservatism and prejudice.

In Bombay I engaged a man-servant to accompany me on a trip to the Punjab. It being a winter of unusual severity, and the journey involving much night travel, the agent from whom I hired the servant advised me that it would be a beneficial as well as a humane act were I to give the man ten rupees with which to procure an "outfit" suitable for one going to the north. "It 's sometimes done, but not often enough to make it a custom," explained the agent; "but it would be the right thing—and because voluntary, the poor fellow should serve you all the better for your generosity. Give him but ten rupees, and see that he spends it all for heavy undergarments and serviceable shoes."

Experiencing some haziness as to how any tittle of reputation for generosity was going to be reared on an expenditure aggregating just $3.20 in American money, I communicated my determination to the man who perforce was to be my constant companion for a month, and who had it in his power to make me love or hate the country. As was to be expected, I was many kinds of a sahib for my munificent benefaction, and Torab Jan salaamed almost to the floor when promising to return from the bazaars in good time to strap my mattress and pack my trunk in readiness to go to the station directly dinner was over.

Hours later, but in time to throw my clothes and books into trunk and bags, Torab stalked into the apartment, and close upon his heels was another native carrying a not overlarge parcel. Torab was frank in stating that he had purchased precisely what he needed, and proffered a snip of paper covered with characters in Hindustani to prove he had expended precisely ten rupees, which made it necessary to have another benefaction—two annas this time.

"What are the two annas for, and who is this man?" I asked.

"He 's the coolie bearing my parcel from the bazaar, master," was the response; "you must know that my caste makes it impossible for me to carry parcels."

"See here, you drooling idiot; what do you think I have hired you for? Why, you 've got to carry parcels, lots of them, and big ones at that; and you 'll have to carry that bed there and my trunk half over India, likely as not. Don't talk to me about caste."

"Pray, master, don't be angry with me. I know I 'm to carry *your* things—that 's what I 'm for. I forgot to explain that my caste forbids only the carrying of my own parcels," the poor fellow whined.

And so it was. In places where there were no carriages Torab seemed to delight in loading himself down with my paraphernalia, but his belongings had always to be carried religiously by a native of a breed earning its living by acting as human drays.

HIS HIGHNESS THE MAHARAJAH OF JEYPORE

CHAPTER VII

THE VICARIOUS MAHARAJAH OF JEYPORE

THOUSANDS of travelers make the pilgrimage to India, a land hoary with age, and when weary of overwrought temples and tombs, when arid plains and malodorous towns lose their power to interest, they journey north to Rajputana to revel in Jeypore, the unique—at least, lovers of Kipling do. And the effect on jaded senses is like a cooling draught after a parching thirst. Kipling called Jeypore "A pink city, to see and puzzle over." It surely is pink, all of it that is not sky-blue, and for various reasons it is more satisfying than any other town in India.

For a land where time is calculated by century units, Jeypore is almost as recent as a "boom" city on an American prairie. As a fact, its first building was reared only a hundred and seventy-eight years ago; and this modernity explains thoroughfares of remarkable breadth that cross each other at right angles. Generations the senior of Jeypore, New York is no better exponent of the checker-board idea. Jeypore is but the setting of a scene harking back to medieval days, however, and is the capital of an independent state greater in area than Belgium, and from its palace and judicial chambers nearly three million souls are governed. Nowhere in India, outside the great Rajputana province, is it possible to view a picture of happy and contented life, and in the city of Jeypore this is seen in its perfection.

This ornate capital on the plains, hemmed in by fortress-crowned hills, is a veritable stronghold of feudal barons and armed retainers, of hermits and monasteries, and is dotted with palaces and public buildings pertaining to the Maharajah's rule. Many of the structures are new enough to suggest what Americans love to call "modern conveniences." The principal streets are broader than Broadway, as well paved, and illuminated by gas systematically enough installed to indicate the presence behind the scenes of European engineers. Strange to say, Jeypore is an Indian city wherein the lordly Briton in khaki is never seen: if the English functionary be here, his master is none other than the Maharajah. Through its streets surge a people almost childish in their happiness, some in ekkas drawn by matched pairs of bullocks, others mounted high on the backs of trotting camels, while bands of chattering Rajputs on foot are omnipresent—every grouping reminds of something witnessed on the stage, and the *tout ensemble* might be the great scene of a realistic opera intended to glorify the people and the institutions of India.

Feminine adornment is carried in Jeypore to its extreme. The bright-hued skirts of the women are flare-fashioned and "fuller," in dressmakers' parlance, than anything dared by Fay Templeton. But the Jeypore beauty's real passion is for gold and silver jewelry, and she carries this to a degree unrivaled by the women of any other section of India. It is not trifling with fact to say that the average Rajput woman wears from eight to ten pounds in silver on ankles and toes, and bracelets enough to sheath arms from wrist to elbow. Every feminine Jeypore nose bears some metal ornamentation—gold studs through the nostrils, and generally a hoop of gold depending a full inch below the point of the chin. Their ears are deformed by the wealth of metal hanging from lobe or strung on the upper rim of that organ. It can be said of Jeypore's fair sex that they are bimetallists in the strictest sense. The argument of the savings-bank has probably never been brought to their attention, for when one of them has a little money ahead she purchases a silver ornament for her person; and if a windfall come to her by legacy or otherwise, she buys something of gold, most likely a necklace of barbaric design. When one of these women goes to the market-place or the public well, she wears everything of value she possesses, and for the best of reasons her home is never pilfered.

Rajput men and women look a visitor in the face, and by their smiling countenances seem to welcome you to their country. They lack the broken-spirited look and sullen servility of Indian peoples overlorded by Thomas Atkins. In Jeypore there are grandees and warriors, painted dogs, hunting leopards, bedecked horses, and hulking elephants in every street picture—and these pictures change with the facility of groupings of the kaleidoscope.

The open-air shops of the metal workers and enamelers, and of the dyers, whose favorite colors are magenta and yellow, are interesting. There, on the left, is the imposing façade of the Palace of the Winds, extolled by Sir Edwin Arnold as "a vision of daring and dainty loveliness," but which in reality is scarcely more than a mask of stucco erected to make a show from the street. The Maharajah's palace and grounds cover a seventh of the area of this finest of modern Hindu cities. A stone's throw from the palace portal is a temple wherein Jeypore women beseech the image of Siva to bless them with children: and elsewhere are a Gate of Rubies, and a Temple of the Sun. At scores of wayside shops tiny idols of the Hindu hierarchy, and silver bracelets and gewgaws, are sold to people almost infantile in their cheerfulness. Wedding processions pass and repass with a frequency proving an active matrimonial market, each led by joyous singers and drum-beaters.

An entrancing place is this seat of His Highness of Jeypore, and compensating for the tedious railway journey from Delhi landing one at the city's gates in the inky darkness of 4:30 in the morning. At his hotel a visitor learns that a formal request must be made for permission to inspect the Maharajah's palace and stables, and to

A MATCHED PAIR OF BULLOCKS, JEYPORE

go to the abandoned capital of the state, Ambir, five miles away. You make application through a deputy, usually the man-servant traveling with you, and an hour later comes formal notification that His Highness welcomes you to his capital, and that a state carriage will be sent for your use, as well as a state elephant to carry you up the hills to Ambir. This outburst of hospitality comes with a surprise and force that almost sweeps one off his feet, and you have instant misgivings for having troubled the august potentate at such an unreasonable morning hour. Then your brain almost reels as you recall books that had dwelt upon the limitless hospitality of Eastern princes, and you hope that His Highness will not insist upon your dining with him—with your evening dress and high hat awaiting you at a Bombay hotel a command to the palace would, to say the least, be awkward.

But you are spared this inconvenience, probably because the Maharajah is as familiar with deputed affairs as you are. Two gaudy chaprassis who have brought the desired permits are His Highness's deputies, and from them you learn that their master has been for a fortnight at Calcutta, but is expected to return in a day or two. They come into your room and assure you in fair English that they are detailed for your use as long as you honor Jeypore with your benevolent presence. They wear curious swords high under the left arm, and beautifully inlaid shields are belted to their right arms—these trappings are badges of office, but you wonder if they would sell them to be taken to America to become conspicuous adornments of somebody's cosy corner.

A person with a fondness for simplicity, or possessing scruples against kingly institutions, may escape the state carriage by despatching a firm and prompt declination of the honor. But the chaprassis remain; and the elephant, already trudging to the base of the Ambir hills to await your coming, cannot be countermanded or headed off. In this charming manner the great Maharajah entertains daily the handful of strangers within his gates—it is India's remaining relic of the hospitality of long ago. A distinction inordinately prized by native princes is the number of guns prescribed by the Indian government as their salutes. The Gaekwar of Baroda and two other feudatory rulers are entitled to twenty-one guns, while the hereditary right of the Maharajah of Jeypore is only seventeen. But the present Maharajah, as a reward for his enlightened administration, is made happy by having four additional guns—and no king or emperor can have higher acclaim from the cannon's mouth.

One cannot tarry a day in Jeypore without hearing redundant testimony that His Highness Sir Sewai Madho Singh is a fine man, devoted to his people and unswervingly loyal to his religion. His visitors are often lords and ladies of England, who find his hospitality as interesting as it is boundless. To the tips of his fingers he is a Hindu devotee with all that the term can mean. When he

STREET SCENE, JEYPORE, SHOWING PALACE OF THE WINDS

attended the coronation of Edward VII, in London, the preparations for his sea-voyage were unprecedented in orthodoxy. An ocean liner was specially chartered for him and his suite; in all one hundred and twenty-five people formed the escort. Six special kitchens were fitted up on the ship, including one to prepare food exclusively for His Highness. There was, as well, a special temple, paved with marble, for the family idol, before which the Maharajah prostrated himself many times daily. Drinking water from the sacred Ganges, and every article of food—enough to sustain the entire party for six months—were carried from India. So rigidly was the orthodoxy observed that even the sand for cleaning cooking utensils was placed on board at Bombay; and washermen, carpenters, blacksmiths, and others accompanied the party, that there be no necessity for purchasing anything in England, or having work done by persons not of the Hindu faith. That the august traveler's caste be untainted, extra tanks of water from Benares were subsequently sent to England by frequent steamers.

The Maharajah maintains a military force of nearly 4,000 cavalry and 16,000 infantrymen. Besides these soldiers, his retainers number thousands, and their right to wear a sword is a coveted distinction throughout Jeypore state.

The palace stables contain three hundred horses, but the equipages and trappings are more interesting than the animals. There are some superb Arab steeds, however. A visitor noting the army of grooms wonders that the management is not better systematized; but a word from your traveling companion, who knows the ways of maharajahs, is to the effect that an Indian nabob is forced by custom to support thousands whether there be work for them or not. His Highness's stables and carriage-houses somehow suggest a circus in winter quarters. The fact is that Jeypore's ruler takes little interest in horseflesh and carriagemakers' creations. His preference is for elephants—animals befitting a dynasty descended from the sun and moon.

"Will the sahibs visit the elephant stable?" The sahibs communicate their desire to do so. Mahouts with pikestaffs lead the way, and a myriad of hangers-on swarm in the train of the visitors. The accoutrements seen en route to the stable are interesting, surely, especially the howdahs. Some of these are of silver. One was used by the Prince of Wales; another was fashioned for the Maharajah's use at the Delhi durbar, and a gorgeous one is reserved for the viceroy whenever that mighty personage pays a state visit to Jeypore. A half-dozen howdahs are specially fitted for the Maharajah's favorite sport, tiger-hunting. Some of the howdah cloths represent a fortune in gold and silver bullion, while a few are saved from tawdriness by the skill of the embroiderer in silk.

The elephants are now trumpeting impatiently for inspection. Their compound is a series of roofless walled enclosures, and a visitor notes with grateful appreciation the strength of the

COURT DANCERS AND MUSICIANS, JEYPORE

chains anchoring the beasts to mother earth. A leviathan is straining at his tether in a mad effort to reach a vagabond who is tantalizing him with a pike, and your guide—one of the official messengers with sword and shield—says: "He no like Hindu people; last week he kill two." Beasts as docile as kittens take nuts from your hand, and evince disappointment when more are not forthcoming. Five magnificent tuskers, that promptly obey their keeper's command, are used by His Highness for tiger-hunting; and a bevy of complaisant elephants, quartered in a single stable, have grown old in carrying tourists up the Ambir hills, it is explained.

From the elephant stables the chaprassis scurry the visitors through fragrant gardens and under bizarre arches to the crocodile department, where a score of saurians are pastured in an enclosure that is half swamp and half lake and is acres in extent. Visitors are placed at the top of a staircase of masonry descending to the water, while two wild-eyed Hindus seek to rouse the crocodiles from their siesta on a grassy islet a hundred yards away by a series of shrieks that would disgust self-respecting animals and reptiles. In a leisurely manner the crocodiles seem to recognize the signal to mean that a new lot of tourists desire to see them fed. It requires a good quarter of an hour for the Indians to lure them to the foot of the staircase, and from the first it is plain that the crocodiles view with indifference your visit to Jeypore. The lower step is finally fringed with opened mouths which in a moment engulf a mass of slaughter-house refuse almost thrust down their throats by the wild-eyed showmen, whom you reward with a shower of rupees which they believe marks your appreciation of their efforts.

As you are whisked through the palace yard, on the way to the carriage, you espy through an open door a splendid room fitted with paraphernalia not associated with medieval pastimes. It is the Maharajah's billiard-room, sumptuously furnished, and filled with tables of the latest English make.

Probably because they are proud of the fact that a former ruler of Jeypore was a generous patron of science, the chaprassis pilot you to the park given over to the apparatus of the celebrated Hindu astronomer and mathematician, Jai Singh. It contains dials, azimuth masonry, altitude pillars, astrolabe, and a double mural quadrant of enormous size and height, on which the gradations have been marked. In a way this exhibit of obsolete paraphernalia refutes the idea that Jeypore's maharajahs have lived solely for the gratification of the senses by amusements. A few minutes later you are at the public tiger-cages, where a dozen bona fide "man-eaters" are lazily stretched in shaded corners of their prison cages. Thirty odd years ago the present King of England killed his first tiger near Jeypore, and the animal ever since has played an important part in the city's pleasures. One inmate of the cages has an authenticated record of ten Indians killed, before His Highness's retainers lured him into ambush and made him a prisoner. "Two days from now," explains one of the men carrying sword and shield, "that tiger there,"—indicating a sullen beast,—"is to fight a wild elephant for the Maharajah's entertainment. Would the sahibs care to witness the combat?" The visitors promptly regret that they have unbreakable engagements in another part of India. Cheetahs are then led forth for admiration. Zoos and menageries know them as leopards—in India they are cheetahs, and are trained to course deer and antelope. A huntsman releases a cheetah, whose gaze has been directed to a fleeing deer on the plain, and in a few minutes the deer is a captive.

So much for the diversions of Jeypore's autocrat.

A distinct touch of beauty is imparted to his capital by the peacocks of imperial strut and plumage. They are everywhere—on the crenelated city wall, in the hurly-burly of the streets and bazaars, even on the steps leading to temples and mosques. The peacock is sacred to Jeypore; it crowns in miniature the street lamps, and is sculptured in hundreds of places. Chattering parrots by the roadside may arrest attention, but are forgotten in a moment—a strutting peacock is beautiful enough to place the parrot family in eclipse. When blue-rock pigeons descend by thousands in the market-place to profit by an over-turned sack of grain, visitors marvel at their irridescent necks and breasts—but a beauteous peacock appearing on the scene attracts an admiration amounting to monopoly.

But the appointment with the state elephant—what of that?

Surely, Ambir must be seen. There it was that all the ancient splendor originated and dwelt for centuries, and until a practical maharajah decided that a mountain retreat was ill-suited to the needs of a capital. The possessor of this astute mind moved himself and his machinery of government to the plain below—and all his people followed. This explains why Ambir is now deserted, and why a court steeped in medievalism has a setting bristling with newness.

Every adjunct of a fortified residence is there in the hills. Miles of battlemented masonry, pierced every few feet for bowmen, surrounds the straggling mass of buildings. Terraces are set upon the mountainside like a gigantic staircase, and fringed with railings of stone so artistically wrought as to suggest the grill-work of the matchless Taj Mahal. Great gray monkeys descend from the mountain slope to feed from the hands of your guides; and they are not of the moth-eaten variety seen in captivity, but are freeborn denizens of the forest, whose coats glisten and whose curly tails are of unusual length.

Some of the apartments in the old palace rival anything to be seen at Lucknow, Agra or Delhi. A gem of a temple, adjoining a public audience hall of marvelous richness in finish, is dedicated to the awful goddess Kali, and each morning a goat is sacrificed to this deity, ever craving blood, by Hindu priests attached to the Maharajah's court. This is a revolting blot on a series of majestic buildings that unite to make one of India's greatest sights.

"How blessed would it be," you meditate, "if the betel-chewing priest might be sacrificed in place of the innocent and helpless animal." But no, human sacrifices are no longer permitted in India; England stopped them years ago.

Oh, yes; the state elephant. Well, it was extremely useful, for it rescued four stalwart native servants, laden with tiffin basket and a dozen bottles of mineral water, from toiling up the hills on foot. Perched on his back like nabobs, they probably indulged in remarks disparaging of their masters, electing to walk, and mused maybe upon the theory that now and then man meets his deserts.

CHAPTER VIII

THE WORLD'S MOST EXQUISITE BUILDING

A MOGUL ruler who did things was Shah Jahan, and he came of a race not content with ordinary achievements. His grandfather, Akbar, was probably the greatest personage ever born in India. He it was "whose saddle was his throne, the canopy of which was the vaulted dome of heaven." Akbar made Eastern history, made it fast, blazoning it with proud records of conquest and empire extension. Akbar was the grandest man who ever ruled Central India, and it was he who developed the Mogul Empire to the loftiest importance it attained.

Shah Jahan embellished the empire with noble structures, and his impulse for building amounted to mania. Time annulled Akbar's achievements, but those of his grandson stand to-day, and the structures of his era are beautiful enough to attract admirers from every corner of the earth. A famous critic once said that Shah Jahan built like a giant and finished like a jeweler. His works have made Agra, of all cities in India, the place of unrivaled interest.

Agra's Taj Mahal is the most exquisite building

THE TAJ MAHAL, AGRA

ever erected by the hands of man, and is a romance as deftly wrought in marble as any writer ever fashioned in words. It marks a great man's love for a woman—Arjamand Banu Begum, his wife. Shah Jahan was a Mohammedan despot who led a magnificent life, and had other wives; but in his eyes the peer of her sex was Arjamand. When she died in giving birth to a child, he declared he would rear to her memory a mausoleum so perfect that it would make men marvel for all time. And this he accomplished. More poetry and prose have been written about the Taj, with more allusions to it as a symbol of love, than of any other creation marking human affection—and the secret probably lies in the fact that all the world loves a lover.

Arjamand had many titles of rank and endearment, but poets like Sir Edwin Arnold preferred to speak of her as Mumtaz-i-Mahal, meaning the "Exalted of the Palace," when extolling the charms of this splendid niece of Nur-Mahal, who likewise had been famed for beauty and charity.

Shah Jahan ruled from 1628 to 1658, and had been on the throne only two years when death took from him his adored Arjamand. Then came the resolve to erect to her memory a monument that might measure his love and grief. Since Akbar's time, the best architects, artists, and skilled workmen of India, Persia, and Arabia had been attracted to Agra and neighboring Delhi. All were summoned to Shah Jahan's court, and the resources of his empire placed at their disposal. The

Taj, consequently, was not the creation of a single master mind, but the consummation of a great art epoch. Its construction was commenced four years after Arjamand's demise.

The bereft emperor had appointed a council of great architects of India to guide the work. Drawings of celebrated structures of the world, especially those in Moslem lands, were studied. More than one European was attracted to the Mogul court, and it is believed that Geronimo Verroneo, who had journeyed from Italy, laid several plans before Shah Jahan. There are records at Agra showing that certain suggestions of the Italian were adopted, but it is common belief that the general design was the recommendation of a Turkish or Persian architect named Ustad Isa.

In keeping with an old Tartar custom, a garden was chosen as the site of the tomb—a garden planted with flowers and fragrant shrubs, emblems of life, and solemn cypresses, emblems of death and eternity. In Mogul days such a garden was maintained as a pleasure ground during the owner's lifetime, and used for his interment when dead.

> "And she who loved her garden, lieth now
> Lapped in a garden.
> And all this for Love!"

The laborers came from many parts of the world—the chief masons from Northern India and Bagdad, the dome builders from Asiatic Turkey, and the mosaic artists from Persia and probably Italy. Every section of India and Central Asia was drawn upon for materials. The marble, spotless in purity, was brought from Jeypore, 300 miles away, on the backs of elephants and camels or by bullock carts. The red sandstone was contributed by Fathpu Sikrij, the jasper by the Punjab, the crystal and jade by China. The turquoises came from Tibet and the Red Sea, the sapphires and lapis lazuli from Ceylon, coral and cornelian from Arabia, onyx and amethysts from Persia, and the diamonds from Bundelkund.

It engaged the unceasing labor of 20,000 men for seventeen years to complete the Taj; and like that other great tomb, the Cheops Pyramid in Egypt, it was reared chiefly by forced labor, unpaid and uncared for, and thereby produced great suffering and mortality. This is the chief blemish attaching to the project that gave to art the mausoleum overlooking the Jumna.

According to native accounts the cost of the Taj was lakhs of rupees having to-day a value of $20,000,000; and local tradition affirms that not half this sum was ever paid by the emperor—this is a blot upon the sincerity and strict uprightness of the magnificent grandson of Akbar.

The Taj garden is perhaps a half mile square, and is surrounded by a strikingly beautiful wall of masonry. It is an orderly wilderness of rich vegetations, to be found only in Asia, and the deep greens and rich browns of the avenues of foliage unquestionably accentuate the whiteness of the

Temple of Death. As the garden helps the tomb, so the tomb gives expression to the garden.

The great gateway of red sandstone, whose roof is adorned by Moorish arches and pavilions, is in itself one of India's most perfect buildings. From its summit a perfect view of the Taj is had, with the Jumna flowing sluggishly beneath its marble platform; and from there the grounds are spread before the visitor in a perfect panorama. The paved avenues, all leading to the magnificent pile, miles of marble acqueducts filled with ornamental fish, playing fountains—all breathe the superlative of art, every fluttering leaf whispers of the East.

Not by its size is Arjamand's tomb commanding, for its dimensions are very moderate. Imagine a plinth of flawless marble, 313 feet square, and rising eighteen feet from the ground—that is the foundation of the wondrous structure. The Taj is 186 feet square, with dome rising to an extreme height of 220 feet; that is all. At each corner of the plinth stands a tapering minaret rearing its crown 137 feet;

> "—four tall court ladies
> tending their princess."

No building carries the idea of personality further than the Taj, a feminine personality, as it should be, for it contains no suggestion of the rugged grandeur of a tomb for a great man. The Taj is the antithesis of Akbar's mausoleum, of the

ALABASTER SCREEN ENCLOSING ARJAMAND'S TOMB, TAJ MAHAL

Parthenon, of Napoleon's resting-place, of Grant's robust mausoleum on the Hudson. A sepulcher fashioned after ordinary architectural canons can only be conventional: the Taj is different from all other buildings in the world; it is symbolical of womanly grace and purity—is the jewel, the ideal itself; is India's noble tribute to the grace of Indian womanhood, a tribute perhaps to the Venus de Milo of the East.

The grace of the Taj, as do the achievements of every form of perfect art, rests in its simplicity. A spectator marvels that so much beauty can come from so little apparent effort. Yet nothing is wanting, there is nothing in excess; we cannot alter a single stone and claim that the result would be better. And Oriental designers, working for an Eastern despot, might easily have struck a jarring note and rendered the Taj garish—the wonder is that they did not. The Taj consequently is the objective of most travelers making the pilgrimage to India.

It is easier to tell what the Taj is than to speculate upon the ideals and motives of its builders, and it should be a brave writer who attempts to describe it. Kipling, who saw the structure first from the window of a train nearing Agra, called it "an opal tinted cloud on the horizon"; and after studying the building at close range he wrote, "Let those who scoff at overmuch enthusiasm look at the Taj and thenceforward be dumb; . . . each must view it for himself with his own eyes, working out his own interpretation of the sight." Another great English writer has said, "Words are worthless in describing a building which is absolutely faultless." And it taxed the talents of Sir Edwin Arnold, critic and poet, to frame in language an adequate picture of Arjamand's death couch.

If a man possesses the sentiment of form and proportion, the Taj will satisfy him. The stately portal seems to harmonize with the grandeur of an Eastern queen; and the aërial dome, higher than its breadth, rests upon its base as if possessing no weight, yet is of solid marble. Heroic in treatment are the quotations from the Koran framing every doorway and aperture, wrought in inlay or sculptured in relief—and these modify the pearly monotony of the marble.

One enters reverently the burial-place of Shah Jahan's queen, whose cenotaph is of the whitest marble, placed in the precise center of the building, and surrounded by an octagonal screen of alabaster that is pierced and interwoven like lace. Every foot of the walls, every column and panel, is elaborately embellished with flowers, leaves, scrolls, and sentences, and these are inlaid in jasper, bloodstone, jade, onyx, and precious stones. Arjamand's tomb blossoms with never-fading Persian flowers and Arabic sentences extolling her character, and is as marvelous in workmanship as if produced by Florentine inlayers of the present time. The sarcophagus was originally inclosed by a fence of gold, studded with gems; but this was early replaced by the screen of marble, local history asserts.

The supposition is that one Austin de Bordeaux, a French goldsmith, who had been summoned to Agra by Shah Jahan to construct the celebrated Peacock throne, had much to do with the treatment of the Taj's interior. The building originally possessed two wonderful silver doors, of his designing, but these were looted by Jat invaders in 1764 and melted down. It is said that eight years were consumed by the artists intrusted with the making and beautifying of Arjamand's cenotaph; and further, that the Koran's every line and every word is reproduced by inlay or relief carving on the interior and exterior of the Taj.

To the left of Arjamand's tomb is that of her lord and lover, its location proving that it was placed there obviously from necessity and as an afterthought. It is a span larger than his consort's stone, and occupies nearly all the space allowed by the position of the grilled inclosure—but is a sentimentally fitting intruder upon the general design.

It is a curious bit of history that Shah Jahan, conscious of triumph as the author of the Taj, long contemplated constructing a similar shrine on the opposite bank of the Jumna, wherein his own body was to be placed. It was to be constructed of dark-colored marble, but otherwise to be a counterpart of Arjamand's tomb. The foundations were placed, and the arangements for supplying labor and materials well advanced, when a son of Jahan—Aurangzeb—who had long plotted for the Mogul throne, secured control of the military forces, and overthrew his father's rule.

Aurangzeb promptly adopted Delhi as his capital, leaving his parent to languish as a political prisoner in the palace within the fort of Agra. In a suite of very small rooms, and attended by a devoted daughter, the great Shah Jahan there dreamed away the last seven years of his life—but these apartments overlooked the Taj Mahal, two miles away, let it be known. The heartbroken Jahan outlived his splendid wife by thirty-seven years.

In this manner destiny willed that two great personages forever lie side by side in death; and consequently the Taj is enriched as a temple of sentiment; but—they do not sleep within the marble caskets the traveler beholds. There is a vault deep underneath the floor, and there, in positions agreeing with the monuments above, are the royal remains enclosed in unornamented masonry.

In Jahan's plan for a somber reproduction of the Taj, a monumental bridge was to span the Jumna and link the shrines of emperor and empress. Instead of this fair dream, there is now only a flat, sandcovered shore, upon which lazy tortoises range themselves under the warming sun, and long-legged water fowl indulge in peaceful meditation and slumber.

The curious acoustics of the Taj are observable to the visitor going often to Arjamand's shrine. A harsh voice is echoed harshly back and ceases quickly; but a woman's tones raised gently

INLAID WORK IN MAUSOLEUM OF ITIMAD-UD-DAULAH, AGRA

in song are echoed many times, diversified and amplified in strange combinations of melody. Such a voice reverberates from every side, seemingly ascends, and its force finally dies away to silence like the notes of a flying wood-dove in a forest.

This gem of Agra is worshiped as fervently by Hindus as by those of the Moslem faith, and Indian artists in a few years almost destroy their eyesight trying to portray in miniature upon ivory the architectural perfection and delicacy of this marvel of the world.

When invading hordes have swept Central India, or alien garrisons been quartered in Agra fort, the Taj has always suffered mutilation. The Mahrattas looted it of everything movable and systematically wrenched precious stones from their places in the design ornamenting the fabric of the interior. After the Mutiny came the redcoated soldier, who relieved the tedium of garrison duty by appropriating any attractive piece of inlay overlooked by the Mahrattas—these pretty bits made interesting souvenirs of India for sending home to the British Isles.

For twenty years the British government has been repairing this desecration, under guidance of its viceroys. The great chamber of the Taj now seems perfect in its embellishment—but there are no diamonds, no rubies, and no emeralds, as of old. Bits of colored glass fill their places.

But the Taj's exterior is to-day as perfect as it could have been two centuries ago; and the dignity and sovereign chastity of its marble surfaces —spoiled by no misplaced ornamentation, and unsullied by vandal—make of this poetic shrine an offering to love surpassed in beauty by nothing in all the world fashioned or reared by man.

Nowheres on God's footstool has any queen such a monument, and it is even more beautiful in the silver dress of moonlight than in the golden robes of the midday sun. By day or night alike it makes an impression on the mind that time can never obliterate. Shah Jahan erected the Jami Masjid mosque at Delhi, and the costly Muti Masjid mosque in Agra Fort, as well as the splendid Khas Mahal, the Diwan-i-ain, and the Diwan-i-khas, likewise in the fort—but more satisfying art is represented in the Taj than in all the other structures of his reign.

CHAPTER IX

BENARES, SACRED CITY OF THE HINDUS

UNIQUE among Indian cities is Benares, and for the Hindu the sacred capital on the Ganges has a significance similar to that of Mecca for the Mohammedan, and a greater attracting power than Jerusalem has for the Christian. Benares is the home and shrine of the complex religion that binds the Hindu nations, and is the very soul and heart of Hinduism.

No other place where men congregate can compete with deified Benares in the matter of divine merit that may be conferred on the pilgrim entering its gates and threading its narrow and filth-smeared streets. There two hundred thousand people live and fatten upon the half million devotees coming annually to the idolatrous fountainhead. The sacred city attracts this tide of pious humanity from all the tribes and nations of many-peopled India: they journey to Benares brimming with love and trustfulness, and after a season spent in her temples, at her shrines, and by her sacred stream, she sends them forth overflowing with merit and zeal, to carry her fame to the outposts of the faith, even to Afghanistan and Baluchistan, and to the nomadic tribes peopling Tibet and other lands beyond the mighty Himalayas.

Somebody with a gift for nebulous mathematics has stated that more than two hundred thousand gods of the Hindu religion are represented at Benares. Whether the count be valid matters little, for the city is pre-eminent as the special domain of the fundamental god of India's slavish religion, Siva, whose ensign—a gilt trident and perforated disk—flashes from the pinnacles of hundreds of temples and palaces. This uncanny city on the Ganges is naturally the Brahmins' paradise, for these devotees constitute a governing force in the city's control, and from this fountain-head spread their influence throughout the land of Hind. These insinuating men of religion line the river bank, and infest the temples, sitting like spiders waiting for their prey. Their emissaries are everywhere in India, promoting pilgrimages, or hovering about the entrances to the city to make certain of the arrival of the unwary enthusiast with well lined purse. Rich and poor, high caste and low, all come to the sacred city. Some travel in state by lordly elephant or camel caravan, others by railway; but none follow a surer avenue to eternal grace than those who plod on foot over the Great Trunk highway, sweeping diagonally across India, after the manner of Kipling's holy man from Thibet whose footsteps were watched over by *Kim.* The "business" of Benares being the bestowal of holiness, the manufacture of brass

SCENE ON THE GANGES, BENARES

goods appealing to tourists is incidental in importance and revenue. No other city of its population can have a more insignificant trade measureable by statistics.

For three miles the religious section of Benares runs along the brow of the plateau overlooking the chocolate-hued stream, and every foot of this distance is curious and interesting. Falling below the disgusting temple resorted to by pilgrims from Nepal, the Hindu region beyond India's frontier and "the snows," is the ghat (a ghat is a large stone stairway descending to the river), where the good Hindu gives his dead to the flames, and the muddy inlet from the Ganges where this occurs is dedicated to Vishnu, "the sleeper on the waters," a name singularly appropriate to a place where the ashes of the dead are consigned to the bosom of "Mother Ganga."

A visitor observes a number of platform-like structures of masonry that are decorated with roughly carved figures of men and women standing hand in hand. Upon these, until British rule put a stop to the custom, thousands of fanatical wives underwent suttee and were burned alive with their dead husbands. It is but seldom that a cremation is not in progress at the burning ghat. From the deck of a native boat moored not forty feet away I saw in a single hour eight corpses in varying stages of consumption by fire. The traveler hardened to gruesome spectacles by much journeying in Africa and Asia experiences but little of the sickening sensation through witnessing a primitive incineration at Benares that is caused by a visit to the Parsee towers at Bombay. The Benares operation is sanitary and practical, and something may be said on the side of sentimental appropriateness in having a corpse borne to the riverside by one's relatives and friends, and there consumed by the burning of a pyre constructed by the hands of these. The dramatic entities become apparent to every thoughtful spectator, probably.

A clatter of brass cymbals reaches the ear, and a cortège appears at the top of the ghat, while desultory cries of "*Rama, nama, satya hai*"—"the name of Rama is true"—are heard. The corpse, fastened upon a simple bier of bamboo sticks and carried on the shoulders of four relatives, is swathed in white if a male, or in red if a female. The bearers hasten almost frantically down the decline and clumsily drop their burden in the water, feet foremost, and make certain that the current will have undisturbed play upon the corpse without sweeping it away. The mourners repair to the place where dry wood is sold and enter upon spirited bargaining for fuel sufficient to consume their relative, whose body is being laved and cleansed of spiritual imperfections not a few rods away by the sacred Ganges. Only six or eight logs are required. The dealer demands three rupees for them—and the grief-stricken Hindus offer one. A bargain is finally struck at two rupees, with a stick of sandal-wood for the head of the pyre thrown in.

The logs are quickly conveyed to the burning-

BENARES BURNING GHAT, WITH CORPSES BEING PURIFIED IN THE GANGES

ground, a satisfactory site for the sad office is expeditiously chosen, and the mourners with their own hands construct the pile. Now sanctified by Mother Ganga, the corpse is fetched from the strand and placed on the structure, feet ever directed toward the precious river. The pyre is soon ready for the torch, and here occurs a curious incident, one that illustrates the monopolistic importance of a man wearing only a loin-cloth, who has been taking an indifferent interest in the proceedings from an elevation close by. He is a Dom, of a caste so degraded that should he inadvertently touch a corpse it would be contaminated beyond remedy. But immemorial custom requires that the fire be obtained from him, and he may demand payment therefor in keeping with his estimate of the worldly position of the applicants. Ordinarily a rupee is sufficient, although for a grandee's cremation a fee of a thousand rupees has sometimes been demanded and paid

The dicker with the Dom being concluded, the chief mourner lights a handful of dried reeds at his fire, hurries to the waiting pyre, walks seven times around it, and with the blazing reeds held in the right hand lights the mass at head and foot. The mourners then withdraw to a shaded spot beside a suttee structure, and silently watch the conflagration. In an hour all is over, and the ashes then are strewn far out on the surface of the Ganges and are borne from sight by the current.

From ten to fifteen corpses are disposed of at the burning-ghat daily, and several cremations are usually simultaneously in process. Now and then there is some demonstration of grief, but not often. I saw two men wade to a body in the river, when they pulled away the covering from the face and bathed it with handfuls of water scooped from beloved Ganga, and their every movement denoted affection. Again, I witnessed a tottering and sobbing old man place with every expression of tenderness a garland of yellow and white flowers about the neck of a corpse swathed in red, and imagined it the last office of love to an idolized daughter. I also observed the bare corpse of a man who an hour before had died of plague brought to the ghat by two public scavengers, and committed to the flames of a few logs much too short, until the slender legs had been doubled beneath the body. No sandal-wood perfumed this pauper's pyre, and no interment in potter's field was ever more perfunctory than his burning.

Social distinctions are as marked at the Benares burning-ghat as in the modern American cemetery. An hour spent on the Ganges bank supplies sufficient food to the mind for weeks of serious reflection.

One of the greatest spectacles of India is that of pilgrims bathing in the Ganges. From several ghats devoted to sacred ablutions numerous wooden piers extend into the worshiped stream, and these teem with pilgrims from every section of Hindustan, in every variety of costume, every stage of dress and undress, there to purge themselves of unclean thoughts and wicked deeds, and to wash away bodily impurities. Preaching canopies, shrines for rich and powerful rajahs, and stone recesses for those demanding solitary meditation, make of the river front a place literally teeming with humanity. Devotees are everywhere. Here a pundit is reading the holy law to a half hundred approving Hindus; there a stately chieftain from remote Kashmir ceaselessly mutters prayers beneath a huge spreading umbrella of thatched straw, hired from a Brahmin for an hour; and ten feet away a holy ascetic, naked in the scorching sun, smears his skin with the gray ashes of penitence.

Below this grotesque medley is the multitude of men, women and children, breast deep in the sanctifying Ganges. Thousands have come on foot from far-away villages of this boundless land of paganism; and from all goes up a continuous murmur of prayer and adoration, like a moaning wind emerging from a distant forest. Eye and ear alike are flooded with an indescribable rush of sensations, and the heart is oppressed with the august meanings which lie behind the awe-inspiring sight. All the Hindu cults are here—the Ganges welds them in her holy embrace. But conspicuous above all others is the Brahmin priest, attracting annas and rupees in devious ways from enthusiasts dazed by the realization that they have bathed in Mother Ganga—some want a certificate of purity, others want seals placed on vessels of water to be carried to loved ones suffering from infirmities. The Brahmin gives certificate, places seals, and performs other acts enabling him to garner a harvest of silver and gold.

Now and again a moribund believer, whose friends seek for him something that may be construed as a last blessing, is hurried to the river's edge. It is a sacrament that cannot be delayed many minutes—and the Brahmin fortunate enough to be appealed to charges at emergency rates. When business slackens this harpy composes his nearly-naked body on a plank overlapping the river, and executes with studied deliberation a program of purification marvelous in detail. Receptacles of brass and silver are brought him, and for an hour or longer he rubs his handsome frame with unguents and perfumes, slowly stripes forehead, biceps and breast with the ash-marks of sanctity, and places a wafer of his caste on his forehead. Later he climbs the ghat to his favorite temple, probably content with the emoluments thrust upon him at the water side, or may be he goes to the bazaar to learn the latest gossip of religious and political India. It is in no sense a losing game to be a member of the Brahministic ring controlling things in Benares, for the flow of coin from the two hundred million Hindus is ceaseless.

A curious sight in Benares is the Monkey Temple, a pretentious and not inartistic structure of carved red sandstone dedicated to Kali, the goddess wife of Siva. The image of Kali within the temple is a black fury of hideous countenance, whose red tongue droops to the waist. She is dripping with blood, and crowned with snakes, while

BENARES HOLY MEN

hanging from her neck is a garland of human skulls. Kali wants blood, and if not propitiated daily therewith something horrible is expected to happen. Every Indian town has a temple to this monster; and everywhere throughout what Kipling calls "the great, gray, formless India," sacrifices are made each morning to this ogress with insatiable appetite for blood.

The entrance to the Monkey Temple is slime-covered and the air heavy with sickening odors. Through a stone doorway the goddess may be seen enshrined, grinning demoniacally. Twenty horrible men, harmonizing in appearance to a reader's conception of thugs, gather in the court, to give each batch of visitors the performance that most have come to witness. The frontal region of their heads is shaven smooth, and each loathsome Indian drools betel-nut saliva that looks like blood. A goat is led into the enclosure and tied to a stone post, and the evil-looking men form a circle about the helpless animal. One of them holds the rear legs of the beast clear of the ground. A chant issues from the betel-stained mouths, and a human fiend forces through the circle, brandishing a straight-bladed sword, heavy and keen-edged, that has just been blessed before the altar of Kali. He is the official executioner.

This functionary makes a sign of readiness, swings the blade at arm's length for a moment—and lands a blow on the underside of the animal's throat that severs the head from the body. The gushing blood is directed to the Siva emblem close by, the head is borne triumphantly to the feet of Kali, and each thug-looking man smears his face with blood taken from the Siva symbol, and then dances madly around the carcass. Assuming that the spectacle has favorably impressed the visitor, the high executioner begs a donation with which to purchase a goat for a second sacrifice. You decline, probably feeling that you would subscribe bountifully if a priest might be substituted for the helpless beast.

On important days in the Hindu calendar many goats and sheep are sacrificed, and sometimes buffaloes as well. In time of pestilence or famine it is not unusual to find a child's head deposited in the early morn at Kali's feet, it is claimed.

The inner court of the Monkey Temple, like the ceremony of the slaughter, is open to the heavens, and is surrounded by a cloister lined with cell-like niches for solitary meditation and introspection. On the terrace, on every protruding bit of architecture, on every window ledge—wherever foothold may be gained—are monkeys, loathsomely fat, and made more disgusting from years of pampering than are the human freaks on the pavement. Great tamarind trees overhanging the temple are alive with monkeys. They drop to the ground, run between your legs, and dash before you at every turning. You are entreated to pay for basins of parched corn thrown to the revolting creatures by your priestly guide, and do so, but are glad when the monkeys show their appreciation from a distance. From three to four hundred of these mangy animals belong to the temple, and are held to be sacred. At Benares everything specially nasty or repulsive is protected by the cloak of sanctity.

You are glad to get back to your carriage, so thankful that you throw a couple of rupees to the mob of appealing "priests," in your heart possibly wishing that the money might be invested in soap and scrubbing brushes—and in poison for the monkeys. Urging the coachman to drive speedily for the open space and pure air of Benares cantonments, you wonder as you proceed what place in religion can reasonably be occupied by the revolting customs and beings to be witnessed at the Monkey Temple, and it is with no regret that you learn from eminent authority that in less than a hundred years every temple and shrine perched on the brink of the plateau crowning the Ganges will be undermined and its descent not arrested until the structure reaches the river's bed. Those responsible for locating Benares on the outer periphery of a great bend in the Ganges proved themselves to possess no engineering foresight. But India's controlling religion can receive no setback by the destruction of a few score tawdry buildings consecrated to its gods, for they will be replaced by better shrines and temples, rising from places beyond even the iconoclasm of the sacred Ganges.

Investigation reveals sufficient merit in the religio-philosophies of Mohammedanism and Buddhism to explain their adoption by teeming millions. Each faith offers admirable precepts and teachings, and prolonged study of them produces a feeling of respect for all true believers. But a season of travel in India, entered upon with the desire to dispassionately study the Hindu religion in the land of its overweening strength, produces only bewilderment and mental nausea. The more determined one may be to lay bare the gems of this faith and its administration by the Brahmins, the keener will be his disappointment, for not a redeeming feature will he find, and he may quit India smarting with regret over wasted time. To such an investigator Hinduism must forever be remembered as paganism steeped in idolatry. More, its gruesome sacrifices will provoke only disgust, perhaps equaled by that called forth by the unspeakably coarse temple carvings and ornamentation of the cars of juggernaut. I have been acquainted with Indian gentlemen proud to be known as Hindus, and have been amazed to hear them avow devotion to the hideous idolatry that absorbs a great part of the time of two hundred million people in India alone. If the strong arm of England were not raised over the great empire of the East the suttee rite and child sacrifice would unquestionably prevail to-day. To a westerner Hinduism seems the greatest abomination of the earth.

A BRAHMIN PRIEST

CHAPTER X

INDIA'S MODERN CAPITAL

KIPLING, who has gracefully lured roamers to India by saying, "It is good for every man to see some little of the great Indian Empire and the strange folk who move about it," obligingly prepares those entering by the gateway of Calcutta for an olfactory affront. The stenches of Calcutta are numerous and pervading, surely; but the tourist who has crawled up the Bay of Bengal in a caravel of the Peninsular & Oriental Company cheerfully accepts them. The "P. & O." line is one of Britain's venerated institutions; consequently English people would as soon commit a felony as criticize this antiquated concern. In these times ten-knot passenger steamers are hard to find outside the Calcutta service of the "P. & O." Company and in marine junk yards.

As a great commercial port, Calcutta is unfortunately located. It is on the Hooghly river, one of the outlets of the sacred Ganges, and ninety miles from its mouth. The Hooghly is a tortuous stream of mud that can be navigated by large vessels only by daylight and with favoring conditions of tide, for its channel is seldom two days alike.

This demands expert piloting, and explains why Hooghly pilots are selected with great caution. A Hooghly pilot is the very maximum of a nautical swell, and one's boarding of a ship attended by man-servant and a mass of belongings partakes somewhat of the character of a function.

This Calcutta pilot is a fine fellow—well-bred, educated, and entitled to the splendid compensation and social position which he enjoys. Since the days of the East India Company, the forerunner of British rule in India, the pilots of the Hooghly have been esteemed as personages and they have taken rank but slightly lower than officers of the navy, and much ahead of ordinary commercial people and mariners. When off duty in Calcutta the pilot goes to his club and drives on the Maidan with other Anglo-Indians of quality, and never is seen about hotel bars and cafés like the ruck of seafaring men having a spare day on shore.

The Hooghly is charted practically every twenty-four hours, and on his way upstream the pilot gets his information pertaining to depths and bars by signals from stations on shore. The river presents nothing of interest to the traveler until a point twenty miles from Calcutta is reached; thereafter it is a stream of many attractions. Fortifications with visible native troops and an occasional red-coated English soldier occur frequently; then come scores of enormous cotton and jute mills, attended by strange-looking stern-wheel steamboats, most of them with huge cargo barges

A CALCUTTA NAUTCH DANCER

on either side. At last Calcutta is in sight. Tall factory chimneys and domed public buildings pronounce it a city of size and importance. The last two miles of the journey are made through a flotilla of shipping, a bewildering medley of sailing vessels and steamers, flying the flags of all the maritime nations of the earth—all but the Stars and Stripes of Uncle Sam.

Bombay, on the other side of India, and immediately on the sea, would make a better capital than Calcutta. But the malodorous city of the Hooghly will probably ever be the seat of Britain's rule.

While the names of Warren Hastings and Clive dominate the printed page dealing with modern India, Calcutta fairly throbs with recollections of Job Charnock, the audacious Englishman who raised the red flag of Britain just two hundred and seventeen years ago over a collection of mud hovels and straw huts on the site of what to-day is the capital of the Indian Empire.

Charnock, perhaps the founder of England's rule in the East, was the agent of the old East Indian Company. Having been granted permission by the Mogul rulers to establish a post on the Hooghly convenient for trading purposes, he chose a spot having the advantage of a generous shade tree. The spot and neighborhood now is Calcutta, the chief city of India, with over a million inhabitants. A Hindu village in the vicinity of the place where Charnock established his trading post was called Khali-ghat—these words, corrupted by use, have come to mean "Calcutta." The quaint pioneer obviously had no realization of the part he was playing in empire-making, and Great Britain has never made adequate acknowledgment of the gratitude clearly this man's due. Calcutta residents delight to recount Charnock's exploits, and they take visitors to St. John's churchyard to view the substantial monument beneath which rest his bones. The inscription states that he died January 10, 1693.

A single story proves Charnock's independence of character. He went with his ordinary guard of soldiers to witness the burning of the body of a Hindu grandee, whose wife was reputed more than passing fair. It was known that the rite of the suttee was to be performed—the widow was to sacrifice herself upon the blazing pyre of the deceased, in keeping with Hindu custom. Charnock was so impressed by the young widow's charms that he ordered his soldiers to rescue her and by force take her to his home. They were speedily married, had several children and lived happily for many years. Instead of converting her to Christianity, she made him a proselyte to paganism, and the only shred of Christianity thereafter remarkable in him was the burying of her decently when she was removed by death; but Charnock is said to have observed in true pagan manner each anniversary of her demise, even to making animal sacrifices before the image of the goddess Khali.

Calcutta has improved greatly since Kipling

GENERAL POST-OFFICE, CALCUTTA

wrote of it as the "City of Dreadful Night"; but it is yet a place of striking contrasts, of official splendor and native squalor, of garish palaces abutting in rear allies upon filthy hovels. The good is extremely good—that is for the British official; the bad is worse than awful—and that is for the native.

Viewed superficially, Calcutta looks like a prosperous city in Europe, perhaps in England; but rear streets and suburbs are as filthy and congested as any town in vast India. What the average tourist beholds is spick and span in a modern sense; and what he does n't see is intensely Asiatic, with all that the word can mean. Being a city of extremes, the visitor may be brought to his front windows by the warning cries of the footmen of a sojourning maharajah driving in state to a function, while through the rear windows float the plaintive notes of the muezzin calling the faithful to prayers from the minaret of a Mohammedan mosque close by.

The Indian metropolis presents an array of fine homes, bungalows and stucco villas, put up when the rupee was worth two shillings and a penny, wherein unhappiness may now dwell, because the rupee has depreciated to a shilling and fourpence. The parade of fashion on the Maidan late in the afternoon presents every variety of equipage and livery known to the East. The horse-flesh of Calcutta is uniformly fine. Better animals than are daily grouped around the band stand, or along the rail of the race-course, cannot be found short of

Europe. The viceroy is often seen driving a mail phaeton, preceded by two native lancers and followed by four others. The automobile has many devotees in Calcutta, and bicycle-riding natives are everywhere. The babu is exceedingly fond of wheeling on the Maidan whenever he can escape from his account books. Nearly every carriage on the Maidan in the afternoon has two men on the box and two footmen behind, all gorgeously dressed—servants are cheap in India. At sundown nowadays half the pianos in Chowringee—where Calcutta's officials and prosperous commercial people reside—seem to be playing airs from American light operas, and not infrequently a regimental band compliments the United States by playing "Hiawatha" or one of Sousa's compositions.

It is compensating to a person burdened with the habit of wondering where words come from, to discover that Dum-dum is a suburb of Calcutta, and is important as a military post and as the seat of an ammunition factory and arsenal.

The sights of Calcutta are unimportant. The general post-office occupies the site of the native prison whose horrors of the Black Hole stain chapters of Indian history; and a description of the burning of human bodies on the bank of the Hooghly, and of the animal sacrifices at the old Hindu temple at Khali-ghat, would be disagreeably gruesome. The gaudy Jain temple interests for a few minutes, and the exterior of Fort William impresses the casual spectator. The zoölogical

SHIPPING ON THE HOOGHLY, CALCUTTA

garden is conventional, and the feature of the botanical garden is probably the largest banyan tree in the world. Calcutta hotels, deplorably poor, have been fitly described as of two kinds—bad and adjectively bad. All that interests the visitor within the modern capital of ancient India is the movement of official and social life, and the parade of races forming the population of the marvelous, mysterious country.

There, across the esplanade, with imposing gates and approaches, is Government House, winter seat of the Viceroy of India—whose most distinguished incumbent in recent years was His Excellency the Right Honorable the Baron Curzon of Kedleston, P. C., G. M. S. I., G. M. I. E., etc., etc. Few traveling Americans had the time to speak of him in a manner honoring all these designations. Visitors from Chicago used to refer to him, it was claimed, with naïve simplicity as "Mary Leiter's husband," and let it go at that. A person of extraordinary ability was this husband of an American queen, and it is generally believed that he may some day be prime minister of England. The viceroyship is the highest appointive office in the world. Its compensation is the equivalent of $80,000 per annum, but the allowances for entertaining European functionaries, an army of native servants, and a stableful of horses and elephants for State ceremonials, swells the amount two or threefold. Both at Government House in Calcutta and at the summer home in Simla the viceroy is surrounded by a court equalled in splendor by few royalties in Europe. Compared with the increment and disbursements of India's viceroy, those of the President of the United States appear insignificant. But oriental show and parade are expensive, so expensive in fact, that a viceroy is forced to make liberal drafts upon his private purse.

India may have had as capable rulers in the past as Lord Curzon, but rarely one more tactful or courageous, and never one having the assistance of a vicereine possessing the charm and lovable qualities of the late Lady Curzon. Her splendid work in behalf of the natives, especially the women, endeared her to all Indians. The Delhi durbar in 1903 honored Edward VII in a degree unsurpassed, but was a greater personal triumph for Viceroy Curzon and his accomplished consort from Chicago. His administration had many perplexing situations to deal with and one of them forced his resignation. The constant nightmare of a viceroy of India is famine, and twice Lord Curzon had to deal with this—one visitation alone cost the Indian Government fifty million pounds sterling. His understanding of frontier technicalities, and the ways and wiles of native rulers none too loyal to British rule, assisted mightily in the successful administration of his high office. Under the Curzons' régime Government House balls and garden parties were counted the most brilliant occurring in the East.

A mighty personage in present-day Calcutta is General Viscount Kitchener, commander-in-chief of the Indian army. In Egypt he reformed the nature of the Nile peasant to the extent of making good fighters of the sons of the cravens of Tel-el-Kebir; good enough, when led by British officers, to annihilate the army of the Khalifa; and in South Africa Kitchener wound up with success a war that had been horribly bungled by others. Military critics had long been aware that the army of India was antiquated, honeycombed with dry-rot, and largely ruled by favorites sitting in high places at Whitehall. Consequently, Kitchener was sent to India with instructions conferring almost plenary power to reorganize the forces, British as well as native. He prefers work to participating in the social game.

In England there is a growing desire that finds expression frequently in the newspapers for Kitchener's translation from Calcutta to the War Office in London, from whence the British army as a whole might profit by the trenchant efforts of the Irish soldier who has seldom blundered. As commander in India Lord Kitchener is paid a lakh of rupees a year—$32,000, and heads an army of 242,000 men—77,000 British and 165,000 native troops.

The lieutenant-governor of Bengal, always spoken of as the "L. G." resides in Calcutta and works in close relationship with the viceroy. This British functionary administers the affairs of a territory but one twentieth the area of the United States, but which possesses 75,000,000 people.

And what is this India, governed by Great Britain through its delegated officials? It is a country greater than all Europe, omitting Russia, and fully half as large as the United States. Its population numbers 300,000,000, and is the most heterogeneous of any land in the world—were there homogeneity, or anything approaching it, a mere handful of Britons could not hope to control a fifth part of the people of the earth. India is made up of a multiplicity of races and tribes, professing every religion of paganism; and these are separated by thousands upon thousands of castes each going its own distinct and peculiar way. Great Britain's control of these teeming millions is unique in the history of oversea rule. India is almost exclusively agricultural, and in sections of Bengal averages 900 people to the square mile. At the beginning of 1906 the government had brought 14,000,000 acres of waste land under cultivation by irrigation upon an expenditure of $135,000,000. India now has 215 cotton mills, which employ a capital of $70,000,000, and last year's jute product of Bengal alone was valued at $70,000,000. The Indian Empire is ponderous and complex from any point of view. Possessing but half the area of the United States, it represents one seventh of the British Empire, and more than seven times the combined population of Great Britain and Ireland. It should not be assumed that the whole of India is under British rule, for practically a third of the country is still governed by independent native princes. With almost four times the population of the United

CALCUTTA COOLIES

States, India supports less than 29,000 miles of railway, as against 215,000 miles in the great republic—and this difference makes the contrast between Asiatic conservatism and New World progress.

The person demanding physical statistics gets enough pabulum in a day's search to keep the machinery of the mind going for months, and must be amazed when learning that there are seven hundred and twenty-one distinct languages and dialects spoken in India; that the population has trebled with the British occupation; that for every insane person in India there are thirteen in Europe, —the words "placid East" purveying the explanation. Taking the country by and large it is claimed that only one male in ten and only one female out of a hundred and forty-four, can read and write; and it is said by British residents in the land that the native knows no such thing as scholarship—he learns everything by rote, even to the extent of perfect recitation, without comprehending the meaning of the words he is uttering. It is the nature of illiterate Hindus to resort to the extremest extravagance in nearly every statement, and it is not uncommon for report to have it that an Englishman has spoken abusively of a hundred thousand good Hindus, when that individual has merely intimated to a native servant that he would like his morning meal served with more punctuality. The illiterate Hindu, it is interesting to know, believes that the human soul passes through eight million reincarnations. When this child of the East deals with numbers his tongue runs into meaningless extravagance, and there appears to be no communion between his intellect and speech.

While marriage is universal in India, if not obligatory, the custom forbidding the remarriage of widows works an injustice to the sex amounting to national disgrace. A Hindu maiden who at twelve or thirteen is unmarried brings social obloquy on her family and entails retrospective damnation on three generations of ancestors. A Hindu man must marry and beget children to make certain of his funeral rites, lest his spirit wander uneasily in the waste places of the earth or be precipitated into the temporary hell called *Put*. The last available census discloses the astonishing fact that there are twenty-six million widows in India, meaning that out of every hundred women at least fourteen have been bereft of their husbands, and consequently are no better than human derelicts upon the earth. It is a teaching of the abominable Hindu faith that the bridegroom cometh but once. A pundit of the belief will argue that the practical reason for prohibiting remarriage is to prevent the crowding of the marriage market—and this is the only "reason" that can be extracted from one claiming to speak with knowledge on the unfortunate subject. The enlightened Gaekwar of Baroda, devoting influence and fortune to the moral uplifting of the people of his land, pronounces the custom forbidding the remarriage of widows to be a national curse exceeded only by that compassed by the word "caste."

A statistical paper on India issued recently by the British Government shows that there were killed in that country last year by snakes and wild beasts 24,034 persons—21,880 by snake bites, 796 by tigers, 399 by leopards, and the rest by other animals. The number of cattle destroyed by snakes and wild beasts was 98,582.

The other side of the account shows that 65,146 snakes and 16,121 wild animals were killed, for which rewards aggregating $37,000 were paid.

CHAPTER XI

ISLAND LINKS IN BRITAIN'S CHAIN OF EMPIRE

IF one be a sufferer from anglophobia, a tour of the globe by conventional paths may produce rather more irritation than is good for man—to such a traveler the British Empire is a chronic nightmare, for the red flag is everywhere. Every harbor seems choked with English shipping, if not guarded by a British warship; and Tommy Atkins is the first man met ashore. If your prejudice against Great Britain be unjustly conceived, you will probably revise your judgment before the earth is half circled; at least you must confess that Britain is great from the standpoint of area.

A globe-trotter who has had "Britannia Rules the Wave" ringing in his ears from Gibraltar to Ceylon, connects again with the "thin red line" the moment his ship emerges from the Bay of Bengal. Penang then is the link in the interminable chain of colonies upon which the sun never sets. "Well, this is but an island, and a small one at that; consequently I won't let it worry me," soliloquizes the anglophobe.

Penang is doubly remarkable. Firstly, the tourist is there made to understand that he has finished with that great division of the earth known as "the East," and is at the portal of the Far East, the realm wherein the Chinaman, Malay and Japanese teem in uncounted millions. Besides, Penang is the premier tin port of the universe. Seven tenths of this metal used by the world starts for market from Penang and its neighboring ports in the Malacca Straits.

"Rule Britannia" is played next at Singapore, likewise an island, and, as is Penang, a place almost wholly given over to Chinese and their shops. Few coastal towns in China possess a greater percentage of Celestials than England's city at the tip end of the Malay peninsula and abutting on the equator. Sir Stamford Raffles placed Englishmen—and Chinamen—under everlasting obligation when he brought Singapore into being. Raffles possessed the empire-building instinct, surely, and earned the honor of interment in Westminster Abbey.

Singapore harbor commands one of the greatest natural turnstiles of commerce. Shipping has no other option than to use it. While Englishmen have administered the port and city since Raffles's time, thousands of Chinamen have there waxed extremely fat. The 'rickshaw coolie of Singapore, even, is physically perfect, and consequently in agreeable contrast to the Indian of calfless legs, and his Cingalese colleague of weak lungs. The Chinese 'rickshawman whisks a visitor about Singapore with the stride of a race-horse. For a city only a degree north of the equator, Singapore offers creature comforts in sufficient number to make human existence there extremely attractive.

Nabobs and well-conditioned humanity of Polynesia esteem Singapore much as Europeans and Americans regard Paris—an estimable place of consort, and scores of these men there lead a life not based on the simple ideas of Charles Wagner. Island sultans are usually as numerous in Singapore as princes in Cairo; and European adepts in equatorial government find frequent need of repairing to the gay metropolis of the Straits. An interesting potentate frequently seen is Rajah Brooke, a cultivated Englishman who is philanthropic despot over a slice of Borneo twice the area of England and Wales. Sarawak, his country, has been called the best governed tropical land in the world. Another English celebrity affecting Singapore is Governor Gueritz, administrator of the North Borneo Company, destined, maybe, to become as profitable as the East India Company of old. The Sultan of Sulu (not the hero of George Ade's comic opera) enjoys a sojourn in Singapore. He is young, wears the garb of a Mohammedan who has been to Mecca, and is not displeased by the stare of tourists. The Sultan of Johore, in the hands of money-lenders through unfortunate turf ventures, spends as much time in the city as in his Malay sultanate. A prince of the Siamese king's ministry, in Singapore to bestow orders for bridges and river steamers, goes nightly to witness a feeble production of

HONG KONG HARBOR

"The Girl from Kays," and whistles "Sammy" as he promenades hotel verandas.

Down at the quays great steamships are fed with coal by Chinese coolies who toil silently and expeditiously. A Chinese swell is on the pier superintending the lading of queer-looking cases containing birds' nests, consigned to epicures in Hong Kong and Canton. The Chinaman's greatest dainty is soup made from glutinous birds' nests found in Borneo caves. A single case of moderate dimensions contains nests to the value of twelve hundred Mexican dollars—at least, it is insured for that amount.

Great Britain's next station in the Far East is Hong Kong, likewise an island, and one that might claim the long distance championship as a rain-center. Next to hills, the characterizing feature of Hong Kong is moisture—represented either by rain or humidity. The Briton professes that the climate of this crown colony is good; but for months at a stretch his clothing has to be hung daily in the open air to keep it from becoming water-logged, and everything of leather has to be denuded each morning of green mold. At the hotels one's apparel is kept in a drying-room, and issued costume at a time for use.

The globe-trotter reaching Hong Kong in March risks irreparable injury to his temper, unless he prefers dripping clouds and wet feet to warmth and sunshine. Out of a fortnight there may be a day when the elements will be accommodating enough to allow the glories of the harbor to be seen from the Peak, and two pleasant days in the fortnight would be remarkable. Official figures show that the average March has but twenty-nine and a fraction hours of sunshine. Complain of the rains and the patriotic resident will probably remark: "Rains! These are not rains—they only begin in June." Your book of local information corroborates the resident's statement, for you may read that March ordinarily has a rainfall of but three and a half inches, while June shows twenty, and August twenty-eight. On the 25th of August in 1905 the downpour registered eleven and one-quarter inches—this almost turned Hong Kong into an eastern Venice. November, December, January and February are the pleasant months, statistically, in Hong Kong.

The Briton has displayed his sturdiness of character by forcing a home in Hong Kong, for nature fashioned the north shore of this island to be an abiding-place for birds and animals. Adventurers from the British Isles have won a plateau from the sea by piling and filling in, and by executing engineering feats that have converted a precipitous mountain side to blossom with villa sites and roads and foot-paths leading to them. A railway scaling the mountain height at a topsy-turvy angle did the rest. Hong Kong is a splendid example of what determined men possessed of the colonizing spirit may accomplish. The founders of Venice did no more in the lagoons of the Adriatic. A man responsible for much of Hong Kong's filling in and excavation is Sir Paul Chator, a British

HONG KONG'S MOUNTAINSIDE

subject of Armenian birth, gifted to an unusual degree with foresight. He has done more for the colony than any other person—and Hong Kong has made him a millionaire.

The legal name of the city is Victoria, but this fact apparently is known only to the postmaster and at Government House. Were a visitor to speak of Victoria, the dweller would believe that something back in England, or in Australia, was meant. When China ceded the rocky isle of Hong Kong to Great Britain in 1842 it was the haunt of fisherfolk and pirates prosecuting their callings in the estuary of the Canton River. The acquisition of Hong Kong was due to the refusal of the Chinese to allow British traders to live peaceably at Canton. Driven out of the city, they took temporary refuge in the Portuguese settlement of Macao; but, being pursued by Chinese hostility, the official trade superintendent transferred the English depôt to Hong Kong, which was forthwith occupied by a British expeditionary force, and, at the end of the Opium War, finally ceded to Great Britain by the treaty of Nankin. The name "Hong Kong" is variously interpreted, but the generally accepted meaning is "Fragrant Streams."

Just as Singapore guards the south entrance into the China Sea, so does Hong Kong, fifteen hundred miles away, guard the north. On the south the entrance is through the Straits of Malacca, on the north through the Straits of Formosa. Had Great Britain, according to the usual custom of war, retained possession of Manila, which she had conquered in 1762, instead of giving it back to Spain at the end of the Seven Years' War, her hold of the China Sea would have been as firm to-day as is her hold of the Mediterranean. As the situation now stands, the acquisition of the Philippine Islands gives Uncle Sam a fortified naval base on the flank of the British line of communications between Singapore and Hong Kong. Based on Manila, and given the possession of sufficient naval force, an American admiral can strike right or left, compelling his opponents to fight where it best suits his own purposes. England and America are fortunate in being on terms of complete international amity, but none the less has the conquest of the Philippines by the United States profoundly modified the strategical conditions as they existed in the Pacific when the islands belonged to a weak naval power like Spain.

Hong Kong's population and traffic double every ten years, and no harbor has a greater tonnage. Were Hong Kong a port of origin, instead of a port of call, its commercial importance would be greater than that of London. A few years ago the British Government induced China to lease a slice of the mainland of goodly dimensions, to accommodate Hong Kong's swelling trade. There, a mile and a half across the harbor, to-day stand miles of modern docks and warehouses, and shipyards and engine-building works, that would do credit to Tyne or Clyde. This addition to Hong Kong is called Kowloon, and it has residential districts that range well into the hinterland.

Hong Kong's streets are among the most interesting in the great East, for they strike the key of true cosmopolitanism. Along them 'rickshaws pass in endless procession, electric cars roar, and sedan-chairs swing. The chair borne by four bearers provides the acme of transportation in fine weather. Eighty per cent. of Hong Kong's people are Chinese, and to this multitude the human contributions of Europe and America form necessarily a thin relief. Extremely picturesque are the compradore and taipan in costumes of the richest of silks, more so than is the poor coolie in dirty short trousers and jacket, pigtail coiled for convenience about the head, whose face is none too familiar with soap and water. In and out of the ever-moving multitude glide the tall, bright-eyed sons of India, the Sikhs, who are everywhere in the East. Soldiers in regimentals; jack tars of many nations; policemen, white, yellow, and black, are included in the picture. Here is the somber Britisher with confident stride and air of proprietorship, there the unromantic German slowly but surely capturing Oriental trade. Frenchmen and Scandinavians rub shoulders along the Queen's Road with the matter of fact American and the dark man from Italy; whilst now and then a peculiar gait or unusual costume distinguishes a South American or a son of the Philippines. Here, in short, within this congested square mile of the European quarter are daily to be picked representatives of the world's nations. A study of the crowd is an education in itself.

The splendid buildings speak of commercial prosperity—banks, shops, offices and clubs. Nearly every structure is the seat of prosperous commercial ventures in Hong Kong and China proper; and tiers of water-front warehouses locally called "godowns," are filled with foodstuffs and manufactures that in time will be distributed through every town of importance in the Flowery Kingdom. Hong Kong boasts that her docks can accommodate the largest ships afloat (a fact until the *Minnesota* and *Dakota,* loaded with American flour, vainly sought wharfage), and that she possesses the largest sugar refinery in the world. But these circumstances are subordinate to the British government's real interest in Hong Kong—to make it the base of naval power in Asia, with dockyards and repair-shops equal to any demand, and with coal-bins stacked with the prerequisite to sea-power.

The horse is included in no grouping in Hong Kong, where coolie takes its place as bearer of burdens and hauler of vehicles. The sights of the place are so strange and interesting that a traveler is sometimes there for days before the fact dawns upon his vision that it is a city innocent of horse-flesh. True, there are the runners and polo ponies at Happy Valley race-course. Wherever the Briton plants his abiding-place, there the horse and dog are brought—but in Hong Kong the former requires a deal of attention, for it is only used in making a Briton's holiday. The race-course is set in an intervale, and has cemeteries overlooking

A FORMER "HIS EXCELLENCY THE GOVERNOR" OF HONG KONG

grand-stand and entrances. A transplanted sportsman whose every effort to name a winning steed at a Happy Valley meeting has failed signally, finds superabundance of food for introspection as he runs the gauntlet of cemetery portals on the way back to the city, and very likely indulges in mental speculation as to the purpose in giving the name of Happy Valley to a race-track whose betting ring is overshadowed by burial grounds.

The "chit" as a moral pitfall is more potent in Hong Kong than in India or other Eastern lands possessing a sprinkling of Europeans. A newcomer's ears hear little but "chit." Every sentence uttered by friends, every proposal of obsequious native merchant, is freighted with the little word. You decide at last to cast off your ignorance and be of the elect—to know what chit means and if possible become a chitter. Very disappointed are you when told that chit is simply Asian for memorandum, in popular phrase, an "I O. U.," hurriedly penciled and given in lieu of cash.

Its purpose? Merely to pander to the European's convenience; to differentiate the white man from brown or yellow, by placing him on the unassailable pedestal of a person of honor.

"This chit idea is great," says the newcomer. "I don't load my pockets down with money any more. When I buy a cigar or drink I give a chit, and that 's all there is to it. These Eastern people are away ahead of us in more ways than one." And he hourly signs innocent memoranda, because of the convenience. At hotel and club a chit brings what he wants, it sends a basket of flowers to a charming woman, produces suits of clothing that he does n't need, even pays 'rickshaw and chair coolies.

But alas; pay-day comes at the end of the month! And scheme as he may, the newcomer cannot solve the fiscal problem of making a hundred dollars settle three hundred dollars of debts. He then comprehends that the insidious chit is loaded; is pregnant with the disgrace germ, if he cannot raise the wherewithal to redeem the sheafs of them reposing in a dozen tills—so many notes going to protest with every tick of the clock. "I 'll write home for funds," he decides; "but how am I to live while awaiting the remittance?" By giving more chits, only. He does this with a bold front for another month or so, and is doubly insolvent when the remittance finally comes to hand. Then he gives still more chits, and awaits another money supply.

Hong Kong is filled with unfortunate "remittance men," good fellows at heart, whose downfall dates from their introduction to the chit. A visitor can read no announcement more pathetic than that conspicuously displayed in the waiting-rooms of the Kowloon ferry, saying "Positively no chits received"—and this ruthless pronouncement in connection with a trip costing but the equivalent of three American cents!

There is commendable practicability in the method employed by large hotels in the East for placing patrons in a position to connect with dishes on the bill of fare appealing to their appetites. In Hong Kong hotels, where young Chinamen knowing practically no English are employed as waiters, and where elaborate lists of dishes are the order, the plan is indispensable. It is this: Every dish is indicated on the margin of the card by a number, and instead of saying to the waiter, "Bring me some roast beef, mashed potatoes and a cup of tea," you give the numbers of these several articles, or point to them,—and they are fetched. It is easy enough to get a second helping, but if you desire your meat rare, or well done, or your eggs fried on both sides, then you have good cause for cursing the confounding of tongues at the Tower of Babel. A Hong Kong hotel is not a place for a person predisposed to irritability.

For keen realization of the Far East, Hong Kong, with its streets of Chinese shops, and water front massed with sampans, affords a full and most satisfying opportunity.

CHAPTER XII

CANTON, UNIQUE CITY OF CHINA

IT is a steamboat journey of but ninety miles up the estuary of the Pearl River from Hong Kong to wonderful Canton, and a traveler in Asia who fails to see the city that is the commercial capital of China misses something that he may think and talk of the remainder of his life. Historians profess to trace the origin of Canton to a period antedating the Christian era, when, it is somewhere recorded, the thirty-fourth sovereign of the Chan dynasty, by name Nan Wong, who ruled for nearly sixty years, was on the Chinese throne. In those days the city bore the name of Nan-Woo-Ching, meaning "the Martial City of the South," and was encircled by a stockade formed of bamboos and river mud, tradition has it. Tradition additionally tells us that in the shadowy past Canton used to be known as the "City of the Rams," inasmuch as once upon a time five genii, each mounted on a ram carrying ears of grain in the mouth, rode into the market-place and said to the wondering people, "May famine and dearth never visit your city." This benevolent sentiment uttered, the genii are said to have instantly vanished, leaving their steeds in the market-place, and forthwith these were turned into stone. There is to-day a Temple of the Five Genii, where five clumsily sculptured rams are pointed out as the identical animals that once were flesh and blood.

Passing over twenty centuries we find the metropolis of the present time, with its two million people, the most satisfying, fascinating, and puzzling city in the Orient, if not in the whole world. Canton with its agglomeration of a primitive existence, is surely distinct and different from any other city. Its dazzling color effect, its pile of massive gilding in grotesque ornamentation, its wonderful sign-boards in bewildering hieroglyphics, and its host of odd-looking humanity—all is at variance with anything the traveler has before seen. To successfully view Canton requires some urbanity, a wealth of patience, and a stomach not readily overthrown by gruesome and unusual sights. And, further, the visitor must never forget that his vision is looking back from one to two thousand years, and that the hordes of human beings congesting the labyrinth of streets not seven feet wide, speak of a great nation as it was, which to-day is the oldest living nation on earth. You, of the fast-marching West, are viewing at its fountainhead a race for which the word "conservative" was most likely first called into use. It was the great Li Hung Chang who stingingly rebuked some patronizing Englishmen who were urging the astute old statesman to advocate certain social reforms in China, by saying: "Why, we Chinese look upon England merely as an interesting experiment in civilization, wondering where you 'll be five hundred years hence."

The only impress that Europe and Christianity have visibly made upon Canton is the French cathedral of the twin spires that you see near the place where your steamer lands. In all Canton there is not a wheeled vehicle, street-car, hotel, or mouthful of food appealing to the convenience or appetite of the visitor from the West; and apart from your own coterie of sight-seers, you may for days be about the streets of the vast city without seeing a person wearing the habiliments of Europe. That section of Canton known as Shameen, in reality an island suburb, is set apart under concessions to the United States and certain European powers, and the consuls, missionaries and foreign merchants there dwell surrounded by many of the comforts of home.

Few venture upon leaving Hong Kong for Canton until satisfying reports are received assuring that no immediate outbreak is apprehended of the known Cantonese hatred for foreigners, nor until a vast amount of letter-writing and telegraphing for guide and chair-bearers has been gone through with, and the steamboat company has placed the craft of their line at your command, to be used as hotels, restaurants, and otherwise as bases of supplies. Confident that you would be met at the landing by the guide of whom you had reassuring reports, and with whom you believed you had been in correspondence, a gorgeously-clad, good-look-

TEMPLE OF THE FIVE HUNDRED GENII, CANTON

ing fellow greets you at your state-room door on the boat before your ablutions have been completed, and tells you politely but firmly that he is to be your guide. His card says he is "Ah Cum John," which is not that of the guide you had expected to meet you, and you meekly remonstrate, until the potentate tells you through the half-opened door that you will see Canton under his auspices or not at all. "Why?" "Because I am proprietor of all the sedan-chairs worth riding in, and employ every good coolie; and, besides, Ah Cum, my father, showed Canton to Rudyard Kipling twenty-five years ago. I 'm the third son of Ah Cum, and my family does all the guiding that is done in Canton—nobody else speaks any English."

Whatever your degree of objection to monopolies, a single reason enumerated by the autocrat seeking to enter your employ is sufficient to swing you into a feeble acquiescence, for, to tell the truth, you are not impressed favorably by the mob of jostling, shoving yellow humanity on shore, naked to the waist, who seem to be accentuating with menacing gestures their demands upon your patronage. You wonder how long a white man can be on shore without having his throat cut, and reason that if Ah Cum John can bully a sovereign-born American into accepting him as guide, when you had wanted somebody else, why is he not the very man to control the passions of a fanatical Chinese mob? His administrative ability impresses by the manner in which he directs affairs from the instant his control is confessed by your party of seven native Americans, and after breakfast this born leader sets forth at the head of the timid pleiad longing to explore the great human warren of China—the thugs of the river bank are now your bearers and devoted subjects, four to a chair, and countless assistants and relatives trail at the end of the procession.

The cavalcade attracts good-natured attention from shopkeepers drawn to the fronts of their stalls by the yelping of forty lusty Mongol throats, commanding all and sundry wayfarers to allow honorable visitors to pass. So narrow are the filth-smeared streets that a sight-seer might help himself at will from shops on either side of the way. Hundreds of messes stewing over braziers in the thoroughfare have to be moved, and now and then the bearers of a native dignitary slide into a conveniently wide place that the procession of "foreign devils" may not be inconvenienced. But a mandarin, in his palanquin and preceded by an orderly mounted on a short-legged pony, and guarded front and rear by forty wicked-looking soldiers armed with carbines, has precedence so instantly accorded him that the clients of Ah Cum's third son are almost precipitated sideways into a row of shops. The mighty official passes without so much as casting a glance of compliment at the women of the party, thereby making it evident that Canton mandarins have a code of deportment peculiarly their own.

The products of every section of Asia are said

to be heaped high in the warehouses of this great mart of Southern China; but the tourist sees naught of these. What he views from his sedan-chair is thousands of shops but little larger than catacomb cells, wherein everything from straw sandals for street coolies to jade bracelets for the richly endowed is offered for sale. Preserved from theft and fire in Canton's godowns and pawnshops are stored enough fabrics of silk, art-embroideries, and carvings in ivory and teak-wood, to cause a person of average taste to lose his mind, could they be paraded for his benefit; and a collector would find it difficult to preserve solvency, were the treasures of the shabby-looking warehouses proffered for sale. Unusually repugnant are the stalls where food is vended, for their wares are prepared in a manner making it easy for the visitor to forget that he ever possessed an appetite. A hundred times as you are borne through Canton's streets your chair escapes by only a few feet or inches rows of cooked ducks and pigs that seem to have been finally varnished to make them appeal to the native epicure. Here and there you observe strange hunks of meat held together by a wisp of straw that your guide tells you with immobile countenance are rat hams, and in sundry shops your ready eye thereafter detects tiny dried carcasses that can only be rats. Let it be said in fairness to the sights of Canton that the display of vegetables is attractive enough to turn your thoughts to the dietary benefits of vegetarianism.

You early perceive that Ah Cum John is many kinds of a "boss" by the way he takes command of the shops at which he deigns to halt his caravan. All are charmed with the jewelry fabricated by the workers in kingfishers' feathers, and make liberal selections. But you are not permitted to pay the merchant with whom you have made a bargain, for John says, "You pay him nothing, you pay me to-night for everything"—and the purchases are carried away in his sumptuous palanquin. Pictures executed on rice-paper are next acquired on the same terms; then a cargo of daggers and swords with handles and scabbards covered with shark skin is secured after a brief dicker. When you buy a carved ivory ball representing years of labor by a genius, or a dozen bolts of Chee-fu silk, the price of which may be several hundred Mexican dollars, John insists that you are entitled to a *cumsha* of value. The merchant makes obeisance and proffers you a paper-cutter or a box of candied ginger. John resents this parsimony and says "Not good enough." He goes then behind the counter and pulls down a mandarin coat weighted with embroidery, or maybe an intricately carved puff-box, saying "The merchant gives you this with his compliments." Everything is dumped in the gorgeous palanquin, and your spoliation dash through commercial Canton is resumed.

Between purchases, you are taken to see innumerable temples and other objects of interest, as they fall in your path. The Temple of the Five Hundred Genii is made amusing by the scion of

CITY OF BOATS, CANTON, WHERE GENERATIONS ARE BORN AND DIE

the house of Ah Cum explaining that a figure sculptured with hat of European pattern is "Joss Pau Low." As a reader you are aware that it is the effigy of Marco Polo, the intrepid Italian traveler supposed to have been the first European to have penetrated ancient China. The water-clock, elsewhere, is found to be out of order and not running, and you assume that the water of the Pearl River is too muddy for delicate mechanisms. The execution ground is found to be merely a quadrilateral of vacant land, employed by native potters when not required by the State when a group of criminals is to be officially put to death.

The guide is regretful that your visit is a few days too late for you to see five men beheaded in as many minutes. Employing a chair-coolie as a lay figure, John manages to give a satisfactory description of the *modus operandi* of a decapitation, and you let it go at that. A stalwart native is then introduced as the official headsman, and this functionary promptly tries to sell the heavy-bladed sword with which he says he struck off five heads earlier in the week. Probably three hundred malefactors are annually put to death on this spot, and it is said that the public executioner has been known to sell twice that number of swords in a year. Now and again a loaferish policeman is seen, nearly always leaning against a building or finding support from the angle of a deep-set door. Most of the police wear sandals and straw hats, and carry long batons and revolvers; but there is no sameness of apparel or armament among these guardians of the peace, attested by their wearing only a portion of their uniform at a time. The Cantonese believe their police are equipped and dressed in strict accord with the "finest" of a great city in America.

On the way to that section of the city where Cantonese of high and low degree are laid away after death, we encounter a returning funeral party that made a curious procession, and one stretching to inordinate length. In front was a ragamuffin corps of drummers and men extracting ear-racking noises from metal instruments that looked like flageolets, but were not. Twenty or thirty bedraggled Buddhist priests in pairs trotted behind, proving by their individual gaits that in China there is no union of religion and music. Interspersed in the marching medley were a dozen or more gaudily painted platforms with pole handles, carried by coolies in the way that chairs are borne. Each platform displayed a layout of varnished pigs with immovably staring eyes, plates of uncooked strips of fish, and decorative objects suggesting place in a well-to-do Chinese home. Every fifty yards or so a mustached official of uncertain rank was mounted on a Tartary pony, and at the end of the column a coolie loped along bearing across his naked shoulders the deceased's Yankee-made bicycle. No student of foreign conditions could ask more striking evidence that China was at last "waking up," was heeding the influences of Western civilization, surely. The funeral party suggested perfunctory pomp and display, and gave not a suggestion of bereavement—and that it was, for every person in the cortège was hired for the occasion. Half the food had been left at the tomb for the departed in his spirit form; the remainder was to be devoured by the mercenary mourners when the procession broke up at the door of the home from which the corpse had been carried.

Ah Cum John's clients lunch in the renowned Five-Story Pagoda, rising from the city wall to an elevation that spreads Canton at its feet; but by the time one reaches the building he is satiated with views and wants nothing but food. The Chicago "air-tights" and bottled beers and table-waters fetched from the steamer are relished to the full by appetites not always satisfied by the culinary achievements of a Delmonico.

Travelers insist that Canton is more essentially Chinese in an educational sense than any other city in China. Public speech in Hong Kong reflects the control of Britain, and in Shanghai popular opinion is held to be tainted with German or British opinion. At Pekin the game of diplomacy is played too consummately to allow an expressed utterance to have any national significance, for the capital is looked upon as a city eddying with cross currents and rival influences. Consequently, the pulse of the great Flowery Kingdom, with its more than four hundred million people, can best be taken at Canton, for the native press and native scholars there say frankly what they believe.

Cantonese opinion is potential because the capital city of the great Kwang-tung province is recognized as the center of national learning, where scholarship is prized above riches. No Canton youth who aims at the first social order thinks of setting himself to make money; to enter the service of the government is his object, and to achieve this he studies literature. There is practically no barrier in China to becoming a "literate," and the classification means all that the word "gentleman" can in Europe. For this and other reasons thousands of men in Canton wear horn-rimmed spectacles, look wise, and discuss mundane affairs in a manner brooking no contention. The literary bureaucracy of Canton wields a mighty influence in the affairs of the nation, it is insisted. A member of this class may not be able to do the simplest sum in arithmetic without the assistance of his counting-machine, but he may be able to write an essay on the meanings of ideographs, reproduce a trimetrical classic, or quote the philosophic works of Confucius and the Book of Mencius until you grow faint from listening.

Once every three years Canton teems with men, young and old, who have gathered to compete for academic degrees. Any one save the son of a barber, an actor, or the keeper of a brothel, may enter the list, provided he possesses the certificate of a high school. A certain part of the city not demanded by business or residential purposes is designated as the Examination Hall, where 10,616 cells or compartments are built of brick and wood. These cubicles, six by eight feet square, are arranged in rows, like cattle-pens at an American agricultural fair. Placed side by side they would extend eight miles. These cells have no furnishing whatever, save a plank to serve as desk and bed. The night before the examination is to begin the student is searched, and with writing materials and provisions sufficient for three days, is shut in his cell. This is repeated three times, making the examination extend to nine days. From sunrise to sunset no candidate is permitted to rise from his seat, and if one be taken ill and carried out, he cannot return for that contest. It is said that a few of the old men succumb to the strain at each examination.

The theses or essays of but eighty-three of the competitors can be accepted, and the fortunate ones are rewarded by the Bachelor of Arts degree. In time these compete near Pekin for a "Doctor" degree—and if abundantly rich, the successful scholar may bribe his way to official employment, say persons intimately knowing the customs of China. Those who pass the final degree become members of what is termed the Hon Lum College, and this furnishes China with her councilors, district rulers, and examiners of scholarships in all the provinces—at least in theory. The fortunate man standing at the head of the list in the great examination near Pekin receives the title of Chong Yuen, and is termed "the greatest scholar in the world." The entire empire reveres him, and, taking into consideration the number of the examinations he has stood, he should be respected, if not for erudition, for his tenacity of purpose and the possession of a marvelous constitution. But it is asserted that this "greatest scholar" is invariably a millionaire and a Manchu.

Even the "literate" failing to secure appointment to public office has certain valued exemptions and prerogatives. When he fulminates against the Pekin government or against the acts of an overbearing viceroy, his words are attentively listened to and carry weight. Besides, the horn-rimmed spectacles give him a local standing envied by every man who toils or has to do with business. In Canton and other cities of China, standing before many of the larger and pretentious houses, are ornamental "literary poles," and these are always in pairs and generally show respectable decay. When newly erected they are painted in colors according to the rank of the family—white for a private citizen, red for a civil functionary, and blue for the army. A mast having a single row of brackets a few feet from the top means the degree of Ku Yan, equivalent to our M. A., and called in China the degree of Promoted Men; the degree of Entered Scholar, nearly equivalent to our LL.D., called Tsun Sze, is represented by two rows of brackets; and the highest degree attainable, Hon Lum, is announced by three rows of brackets, locally termed the "Forest of Pencils." The projecting brackets make admirable perches for pigeons and other domesticated birds. As the family and not the individual is the basis of the custom, the masts are always erected in front of the ances-

EXAMINATION BOOTHS, CANTON

tral home, although the distinguished scholar may live miles away. The poles are never repaired or replaced unless some other member of the family acquires academic honors. China has no custom more poetic than the indicating of an abode from which a scholar has emerged.

While it is easy to admit the erudition of the Chinese in their own language, the tourist swung through Canton's streets perceives from his sedan-chair many signs displayed to catch the eye of the foreigner that prove the English schoolmaster to be absent. To read such announcements as "Chinese and Japanese Curious," "Blackwood Furnitures," "Meals at All Day and Night," and "Steam Laundry & Co." provoke a titter in a city where you believe yourself to be an unwelcome visitor. It is obvious that the scholars of China are not reduced to the straits of becoming sign-painters.

The greatest of all Canton sights is undeniably that of life on the boats along the river front, penetrating every creek, and extending along the paddy fields above and below the great city. There has never been a census of this "floating population," but it is estimated that more than three hundred thousand Cantonese have no other homes but the junks, sampans, "flower boats" and "snake boats," upon which they are literally born, reared, married, and die. Lining both sides of the river, extending into Shameen Creek, the sampans are everywhere. They ferry people across the stream or convey them wherever they wish to go in the neighborhood, carry light cargoes of fuel, food, or merchandise, deliver packages, and do a thousand and one services of the "odd-job" order. A sampan nearly always houses an entire family, and is rowed by the father and mother. Beneath the round covering amidships the woman conducts the domestic affairs of the family with a cleverness that is remarkable, and for cleanliness it may be said that the Canton sampan is equal to any abiding-place on shore. The cooking is done forwards over a "fire-box," flowering plants frequently are placed in the boat's stern, and within the cabin incense sticks may nearly always be seen burning before the family idol. A mother ties very young children to the deck by a long cord, while older children romp at large with a bamboo float fastened about their bodies, which serves at once for clothing and life-preserver. It is a common sight to see sampans propelled up and down stream by women, each rower having an infant strapped to her back. The good behavior of the babies of the sampan flotilla is always appreciated by visiting mothers whose nurse-maids at home have difficulty in keeping their young from crying their lungs out.

The "flower boats," moored a mile or two below the business part of Canton's foreshore, are the antithesis of the sampans, for they cater to a pleasure-loving class, to men and women possessing wobbly morals, who love good dinners and suppers and a game of fan-tan without too much publicity, with singing and dancing as adjuncts. In build these craft are like the house-boats of the Thames, and the custom of tricking them out with flowering plants suggests the scene at Henley during regatta week. Practically all the vice that a traveler learns of during a visit to Canton is confined to the flower boats, and their floral appellation comes from the reputed attractiveness of the sirens dwelling upon them. The boats are moored side by side in long rows, with planks leading from one to another. Prices on the boats are always high, and the native voluptuary pays extravagantly and the foreigner ruinously whenever he devotes an evening to the floral fleet. By night the boats are gorgeous with their mirrors and myriad lamps alight, and blackwood tables and stools inlaid with mother-of-pearl; but by the light of day they look tawdry to the point of shabbiness.

To a person interested in marine construction, especially one hailing from a land where steam has supplanted sail-power, and where gasolene and other inexpensive motors have made rowing almost obsolete, the Pearl River "hot-foot" boats, so called by Europeans, are intensely interesting. These craft connect Whampoa and other out-lying towns with Canton, run in and out of rivers, and carry passengers, freight, and sometimes the mails. They are of fairly good lines, but are propelled by huge stern-wheels, and the motive power is contributed by from ten to twenty barebacked and perspiring coolies running up a treadmill that occupies as much room amidships as boiler and engine might. When the taskmaster urges the coolies to do their best, one of these "hot-foot" boats chugs along in calm water at a five-knot gait, but ordinarily three knots an hour is the normal speed.

On the left bank of the river and close to Canton is a large leper village, where all native craft approaching the city have to pay a "Leper toll." If this is done as soon as the vessel reaches the suburb the head leper gives a pass which franks the ship through; without this, any of the numerous lepers are able to demand a fee, which has to be paid, otherwise the junk would be surrounded by these people and all work brought to a standstill.

CHAPTER XIII

MACAO, THE MONTE CARLO OF THE FAR EAST

A PRETTIER marine journey than from Canton to Macao, is not possible in the Orient, and it is of only eighty miles and accomplished by daylight with convenient hours of departure and arrival.

As on all passenger-carrying craft plying the great estuary having Hong Kong and Macao for its base and Canton its apex, you find the native passengers on your boat confined below the deck whereon the state-rooms and dining saloon of European travelers are located, and you perceive racks of Mausers and cutlasses at convenient points of this upper deck. To American eyes it is novel to see every stairway closed by a grated iron door, and a man armed with a carbine on your side of each of these barriers. You perceive on the main deck three or four hundred Chinamen of the coolie class, some playing card games, others smoking metal pipes with diminutive bowls, but most of them slumbering in a variety of grotesque attitudes. None of these Mongols who observe your curiosity seems to hold any feeling of resentment for the effective separation of the races, which places him, the native of the land, in a position that might be called equivocal.

The English skipper and his Scotch engineer, who take the seats of honor when tiffin is served, respond willingly to your appeal for an explanation of the doors of bar-iron and the display of weapons—every first-class passenger always asks the question, and on every trip the British seafarers tell the story of Chinese piracy as practised up to comparatively recent times in the great estuary having a dozen or more names.

And an interesting tale it is, for it recounts deeds of the sea quite as audacious and high-handed as anything performed on land by Jesse James and his stage-coach bandits. Up to fifteen or eighteen years ago the estuary bristled with Chinese pirates, and wherever native fishermen and sailors foregathered, at Hong Kong, Canton or Macao, schemes for holding-up and sacking steamers carrying bullion and valuable merchandise were hatched with a frequency that gave a phase to local commerce that was anything but comforting, and more than one brave Yankee or British sailor went to his death fighting yellow thugs against overwhelming odds. The public decapitation of a handful of these murderers appeared to place no check on the outlawry.

Once a Canton-bound steamer, carrying the mails and a considerable amount of specie, had her progress obstructed by two junks that wilfully forced her into shoal water. In the confusion that followed the grounding, a score of cool-

PRINCIPAL SECTION OF MACAO

ies, who up to that moment had been regarded as honest deck passengers, rushed to the pilot-house and engine-room and murdered every white man on board. Practically everything of value was then transferred to the junks, now conveniently alongside, and the spoil was landed at such points in the estuary that made official detection well-nigh impossible. This is but a sample of the stories you may hear while yellow-faced Chinamen are serving your food, and it must be confessed that it affords a sense of confidence to know that the grates of the stairways are actually locked, and that the rifles of the guards are loaded with ball ammunition. As he sips his black coffee at the termination of luncheon, the captain assures you that until within a few years a skipper was suspicious alike of every native deck passenger and every fishing junk indicating a disposition to claim more than its share of the channel; "but the old days in China," he concludes, "have disappeared forever, and piracy as an occupation has passed with them."

Getting back to the forepart of the ship, the views on land and sea are engrossingly interesting. On the shores of the mainland and on an occasional island are ancient forts which revive memories of interesting experiences of the white man's invasion of the Celestial kingdom, and the foreground of rice-fields is backed by interminable groves of mulberry-trees explaining China's preëminence as a silk producer. Numerous villages are passed, and from them the traveler obtains a fair idea of the rustic life of China. Now and again a pagoda is visible, crowning an elevation, and recalling childhood's school-book illustrations. You jump at the convenient conclusion that these structures of from six to ten stories had to do with the religion of the country, which surmise is erroneous, for the towers were reared to guard the geomantic properties of their respective neighborhoods, and in reality are relics of a bygone age of superstition.

The pioneer European settlement of the Far East—Macao—is at last in sight, and it presents immediately a visual contrast to Canton, by reason of its picturesque situation. There is something about the promontory that takes you back to Southern Europe, to the summer sea and the shores of the Mediterranean, perhaps to a brightly situated fishing port of the littoral of the Riviera. As the vessel rounds the cape and comes to anchor in the pretty crescent formed by the Praia Grande, flanked by terraced houses colored with minor tints of blue and yellow, you know instantly that this stranded Eastern rainbow is Monte Carlo—no, the Oriental equivalent of the beauty-spot of Latin Europe.

Macao is a little place large with history, in fact is an atom of Europe almost lost to public gaze by the vastness of Asia, and as much a part of the kingdom of Portugal as Lisbon itself. As the most enterprising maritime and trading nation of the sixteenth century, the Portuguese were the first to sail the Eastern seas, the first to open up commercial relations between Europe and the great empire of China, and holding the monopoly of all Oriental trade until the end of the eighteenth century. Owing to the prospect of increased gain, following on this European invasion, the waters of the Pearl River estuary soon became infested with pirates, which the Portuguese magnanimously assisted the Chinese government to subdue, and, in return, it is recorded, received in 1557 the cession of the rocky peninsula on which the Portuguese colony now stands. More than once Portugal had to maintain her rights by recourse to arms, but the colony has remained Portuguese without interruption for more than three hundred and fifty years, and is a hoary patriarch beside infantile British Hong Kong and German Tsing-tau. The oldest lighthouse on the coast of China is that of Guia, standing sentinel on the highest point of the Portuguese colony.

The colony has a population of perhaps eighty thousand persons, and practically all these are Chinese. There are, of course, a few score of civil and judicial functionaries springing from the mother-country; and, as in all places where Europeans have long lived in friendly association with Orientals, the Eurasian class is strikingly numerous. In no court on the Tagus are the laws of Portugal construed with more tenacity and precision than in Macao's chambers of justice; and the flag of Portugal floats over the homes of hundreds of loyal subjects who know only in a hazy manner where Portugal really is—they are rich Chinese and others evading the Chinese tax collector, or escaping burdensome laws, and for many years these crafty Mongols have made a sort of political Gretna Green of Macao. Certain influential Chinamen carrying on business in Canton or other southern communities live in almost regal splendor in Macao, and when the minions of the Chinese government attempt to hale them before a tribunal of law, or compel them to share the expense of carrying on the administration of a province, they exclaim in Chinese, "Oh, no; I 'm a subject of the King of Portugal"—and prove it. The great sugar planter of the Hawaiian Islands, Ah Fong, whose Eurasian daughters were beautiful and accomplished enough to find splendid American and European husbands, was a subject of the Portuguese crown, strange to say. His domicile on the Praia Grande is one of Macao's proudest mansions.

The colony of Macao is scarcely more important than one of Anthony Hope's imaginary kingdoms, but for the fact that it is on the map, for the area of Portugal's foothold is not more than two or three miles in length, and a half-mile to a mile in width; it is merely the rocky promontory of the tip end of the island of Heung Shan. A wall of masonry with artistic gateway separates the dominion of Portugal from the great Chinese empire—on one side of the portal the law of the Emperor of China is absolute, and on the other the rule of the monarch of Portugal is sacred. In various ways the

FRONTIER GATE BETWEEN CHINA PROPER AND THE PORTUGUESE COLONY

place and its people remind strongly of a comic-opera setting—but the officer there serving his far-away sovereign discourses with serious countenance of Goa, and Delagoa Bay and Macao as important colonial possessions. Until Hong Kong under the British began to rise as a port and base of commercial distribution, Macao had a considerable trade; but with the decline of business the harbor has silted up until now an oversea ship could not find anchorage. A few industries, like cement making and silk winding, are carried on in the outskirts of the colony, and a suspiciously large amount of prepared opium is shipped, although the closest observer can detect not a poppy under cultivation anywhere on the rocky promontory.

The old Protestant cemetery contains many graves of good men and true, such as naval officers and seamen, who have died on Eastern seas, and whose comrades preferred to leave them interred in Christian soil rather than intrust their cherished remains to cemeteries in pagan lands. The headstones of Macao's God's-acre bear name after name once carried with pride on the rolls of the American, British or French naval and merchantman services, and diplomatic and consular titles are recorded on more than one headstone. It is interesting to scale the steps to inspect closely the façade of the Jesuit church of San Paulo, erected some three hundred years ago. Nothing remains but the towering façade, as erect as if reared yesterday, and bearing silent testimony to the courage of the pioneers in the Far East of the Catholic faith. A 'rickshaw journey through every important street, from the center where are the hotel and government buildings to the remotest patches of farming land near the "frontier," consumes scarcely two hours. In the public park you come not infrequently upon statues with tablets informing all observers of the importance and majesty of the home country welded to the peninsula of Europe, once famed for the intrepidity of its navigators and adventurers. If Macao move the visitor to voice an opinion, it is that under certain conditions which you might name the place could be a veritable paradise, but that benevolent Portugal is there conducting an earthly Nirvana for all and sundry of China's affluent sons mustering the ingenuity and influence to gain shelter beneath the flag of dear old Portugal.

Macao's claim to renown rests chiefly upon the fact that Portugal's greatest bard, Camoens, there wrote in part or its entirety the immortal "Lusiad," which in epic form details the prowess of the sons of ancient Lusitania in Eastern discovery and oversea feats of daring, and in which work the voyages and discoveries of Vasco da Gama are recorded with the fidelity of a history prepared by a sympathetic admirer. As scholars know, the "Lusiad" was first published in 1572, is in ten cantos and 1102 stanzas, and is translated into most modern languages. Important American and English libraries possess it by at least four translators, each being more or less a standard.

BUST OF CAMOENS, MACAO

The life of the great poet is underlaid with romance and sadness. Born at Lisbon about 1524, he was given an education fitting him for a courtier's life, and it was an unfortunate affection for a high-born donna in attendance upon the queen that caused him to be banished from the land of his birth. After a roystering career as a soldier in Africa, he sought shelter at Goa, in India. There he wrote a volume severely castigating the home government for its official abuses in the East, and this led to his being treated by his countrymen as a traitor and outcast. Now in a Goa prison, now at liberty, he at last went to Macao, and it was there that by his pen he redeemed to some extent his good name, to the extent certainly of being permitted to return to Lisbon, and there he died about 1580, poor and neglected. It is insisted that Camoens's influence and efforts preserved the Portuguese language from destruction during the Spanish occupation of the neighboring country, and it is a fact that before 1770 no less than thirty-eight editions of the "Lusiad" were published in Portugal.

To commemorate the eight or ten years he passed in Macao, a public garden is named for him, and there, in a grotto of impressive grandeur, is a bust of the man singing the praises of his natal country as no other writer in verse or prose has ever succeeded in doing. The bronze effigy rests on a plinth upon which is engraved in three languages these lines from the pen of a pilgrim to the Eastern shrine once hallowed by the presence of the bard of a nation:

Gem of the Orient earth and open sea
Macao! that in thy lap and on thy breast
Hast gathered beauties all the loveliest
O'er which the sun smiles in his majesty.

The very clouds that top the mountain crest
Seem to repose there lingering lovingly.
How full of grace the green Cathyan tree
Bends to the breeze and how thy sands are prest
With gentlest waves which ever and anon
Break their awakened furies on thy shore.

. . . . . .

Were these the scenes that poet looked upon,
Whose lyre though known to fame knew misery more?

. . . . . .

They have their glories and earth's diadems
Have nought so bright as genius' gilded gems.

The lines were written by Sir John Bowring, English scholar and traveler, who visited Macao in the latter half of the last century, and the expense of the memorial and its grounds was borne by a patriotic Portuguese, Lorenço Marques, whose name has been preserved by being given to the seaport on Delagoa Bay in Portuguese East Africa.

For a place whose commerce is notoriously in eclipse, you are curious to learn whence springs the golden shower giving the appearance of prosperity to Macao, for the general air of the colony suggests an easy affluence. To keep the governor's palace and the judiciary buildings covered with paint costs something, you know, while the paved streets and bridges and viaducts give support to the surmise of an exchequer not permanently depleted. Portugal, nowadays almost robbing Peter to pay Paul, is in no condition to succor an impecunious colony situated in another hemisphere, you are aware, and you appeal for elucidation of the fiscal problem. "Very easy, dear sir," your cicerone promptly rejoins, "this is the Monte Carlo of the Far East. Gambling is here a business—all the business there is, and the concessions for the fan-tan and lottery monopolies pay for everything, practically making taxation unnecessary."

The statement would cause something of a shock to a guileless stranger, especially to one who had believed he had perceived a natural likeness between the little principality on the Mediterranean and this beauty spot of the Orient. But China is rather too far to the eastward of Suez for simon-pure guile, and the globe-trotter decides to thoroughly explore local conditions by way of adding to his worldly knowledge. If you go to the post-office to mail a letter, you recognize perforce how backward a colony of Portugal may be in supplying the trifling requirements of life, for you stand minutes in a nondescript line before your stamp is sheared from a sheet by a functionary having a capacity for activity possibly rivaled by an Alpine glacier—then you wait at the communal mucilage pot to secure in turn the required adhesive substance. A good correspondent in Macao would pass half his time at the post-office, you conclude.

But there is nothing backward, nothing harking back to the middle ages, in the plan by which the public cash-box is filled, you learn after plodding investigation. The merits of direct and indirect taxation, even of the Henry George program for raising the public wind, have never been seriously considered by Portugal's administrators in the East, nor has municipal ownership of utilities been discussed, you discover. The official bigwigs who administer Macao know that it is as necessary for the Chinaman to gamble as to have food—and the colony accordingly legalizes fan-tan and semi-daily lotteries, supplies the requisite machinery for carrying on the games, and reaps a *benefice* for its enterprise that runs the community without further ado. That is all there is to Macao's fiscal policy. Hong Kong, only forty miles across the estuary, bristles with commercial prosperity. The British government permits Hong Kongers to bet on horse-races, buy and sell stocks, and promote devious companies, but forbids fan-tan and lotteries. There is, consequently, a daily flow of men, women, and dollars between Hong Kong and Macao. Besides, no traveler not actively engaged in uplifting his fellow-man, feels that he has seen the Orient unless he passes a few hours or days in endeavoring to lure fortune at the gambling tables.

The colonial lottery is no more dignified or important than a policy game in an American town, and seems to be but the Western idea clouded by its adaptation to Asiatic uses, tourists affirm.

Macao licenses twenty fan-tan places, and these

run all day and all night, and are graded in their patrons from tourists and natives of fortune and position down to joints admitting 'rickshaw coolies, sailors, and harbor riffraff. The gilded establishment claiming attention from travelers is conducted by a couple of Chinese worthies, by name Ung Hang and Hung Vo, according to the business card deferentially handed you at your hotel, and the signs in front of it and the legends painted on great lanterns proclaim it as a first-chop *Casa de Jogo,* and a gambling-house that is "No. 1" in all respects. The gamesters whose garments proclaim them to be middle-class Chinamen pack themselves like sardines into the room where the table is situated, for they obviously believe in watching their interests at close hand. The floor above, by reason of the rail-protected opening in the center, is little more than a spacious gallery; but it is there that the big gamblers congregate, natives in costly fabrics, and whose rotund bodies tell of lives not spent in toil. They loll on blackwood divans and smoke opium and send their bank-notes and commands to the gambling table by servants, until yielding to the exalted dreams induced by the poppy fumes. They are polite fellows, every man of them, and make it apparent that they would like to do something for the entertainment of each man and woman tourist in the room.

In this strange establishment globe-trotting novices sit around the railed opening and make their bets on the game below through an interpreter attendant. This obliging man lowers your coins to the croupier in a basket, and draws up any "bet" you may have had the luck to win. And what a medley of coins you are paid in! There are coins of China and Japan obsolete years ago in those countries, money of the Philippine Islands, even nickles and dimes whose worth has been stamped by Uncle Sam. It is said that half the pocket-pieces of Asia find their way onto the gambling boards of Macao, and that a thrifty croupier seeks to pay them out to the tourist who will remove them from local circulation. The linguistic representative of the management endeavors to play the bountiful host to most visitors. He takes one through the building, permits you to peep within a chamber filled with oleaginous Chinamen in brocade petticoats, sleeping off the effects of the opium pipe, explains painted fans and other attempts at decoration on the walls, and indicates a retiring room where you may rest or even pass the night, all without charge.

Then he orders refreshments brought, and with the manner of a veteran courtier proffers a tray heaped with oranges, an egg-shell cup filled with tea that is almost without color, and dried watermelon seeds that you might munch after the manner of the neck-or-nothing gamblers on the lower floor. When you politely decline these, the courtly one most likely says, "You no likee tea and seeds—then have whiskysoda." Chinese courtezans, with feet bound to a smallness making locomotion difficult and obviously painful, wearing what in the Western World would be called

IN A FAN-TAN GAMBLING HOUSE, MACAO

"trousers," and invariably bedecked with earrings or bracelets of exquisite jade, edge their way to the gambling table, and put their money down in handfuls as long as it lasts. To spend an evening in the liberally-conducted establishment of Messrs. Ung Hang and Hung Vo is enlightening in various ways.

Because fan-tan is the passion of Asiatics, the popular idea is that it must be the wickedest of all games, if not the most complicated. Fan-tan as a fact is simplicity itself, being no more than the counting off into units of four several quarts of little metal discs called "cash," until there remain one, two, three or four discs. The result determines what bets, laid about a four-sided space on the table, win—a single remaining "cash" makes the 1-side win, two the 2-side, and so on. Each hazard is a one-to-three wager, and the bank pays on this basis after deducting the recognized percentage supporting the establishment. Spinning a top with four numbered sides would accomplish in a minute the same result as the tedious counting of a heap of discs, varying with every "deal" according to the whim or superstition of the players, who may add to or take from the pile prior to the beginning of the count. It is fortunate for the millions of the conservative Far East that their principal gambling game is not a quick one, like roulette, for the player of fan-tan gets "action" only about once in every ten minutes. At roulette and most other games favored by white men a gambler knows his fate in a minute.

CHAPTER XIV

THE KAISER'S PLAY FOR CHINESE TRADE

HAVING no voice in the controversy leading to the war, Germany should have remained neutral throughout the bitter Russo-Japanese conflict. Germany was neutral so far as official proprieties went; but in sympathy and numberless unofficial acts she aided and abetted Russia to a degree unsurpassed by the Bear's plighted ally, France. It is a fact incontrovertible that from the commencement of hostilities the German Emperor was as pro-Russian as any wearer of the Czar's uniform, and most German bankers and ship-owners found it easy to take the cue from Berlin and view situations of international procedure in a manner permitting them to reap golden benefits. Teuton bankers took the lead in financing the Russian cause, and whenever Russia was forced to purchase ships to augment her fleet, these were always found in Germany. When the Czar despatched his squadrons to the Far East, they were coaled practically throughout the long journey from German colliers. And in other helpful ways Germany officiated as the handmaiden of Russia.

The Kaiser's favoritism was infectious throughout his empire, and had the contending armies and fleets in the Far East been equally matched, with the outcome hanging in the balance, the influence of William II could have swayed the continent of Europe in Russia's favor, and a great moral advantage would thereby have accrued to Russia that would have been difficult to overcome. Why? Because the Kaiser is the strongest, most influential, and cleverest potentate in Europe. Splendid exemplar of the war-lord idea, he is really the peer of diplomatists, a ruler whose utterances are to-day weighed and discussed as are those of none other. Understanding the value of words, and a coiner of subtle phrases, an epigram from the Kaiser contrasting the destiny and rights of the "white man" and the "yellow man" would probably have isolated the British as Japan's only sympathizers in the Old World, had it been made at an opportune time.

But the psychological moment never came—there was a hitch somewhere in Asia, and Kuropatkin's genius was expended in masterly retreats; all the triumphs on land and sea were those of the little men under the sun flag. Finally came a mighty engagement, and William hastened to decorate the Russian loser and the Japanese victor. But the point was strained; the public perceived this. As a result, the incident fell flatter than the anticlimax of a melodrama played to empty seats.

The Kaiser's chagrin was great. But it need not have been, for the march of events in the East was proving him simply to be mortal—he had failed to pick the winner, and was gradually becoming aware of it. A plunger in a sporting event perceives an error of judgment in a few minutes, usually. With the War-Lord of Germany it required the lapse of months to convince him of the sad fact that Japan would win in the great struggle.

Why War-Lord, as an appellation for the august William? Adept in the art of warfare he surely is; but have not the Fatherland's victories under his rule been those of peace, and those only? Has Germany been involved in strife possessing the dignity of war since he came to the throne? Has she not, on the other hand, made headway in trade and sea transportation under his guidance that has no parallel in the history of a European state? Yes, emphatically. And are not the words "Made in Germany" so painfully familiar throughout two thirds of the globe, especially in Great Britain and her possessions, that they strike terror to Britons who study with apprehension the statistics of England's waning trade? This is true, also. And Suez Canal returns prove that the users of the waterway under Britain's red flag are yearly less numerous, while the number of German ships is steadily growing.

Then why not Trade-Lord, for this is what the German Emperor is? It is the better appellation, and more truthfully descriptive. It surely is creditable to the German people that their national progress is due to habits of industry and thrift,

TYPICAL BUSINESS STREET IN A CHINESE CITY

rather than to military display: the artisan, not the drill-master, is making Germany great.

And could Trade-Lord William be honestly called "astute" if he overlooked the fact, obvious as a mountain, that one of the stakes in the Russo-Japanese conflict would be the privilege amounting almost to right, to commercially exploit the most populous country on God's footstool—China? More than one fourth of the people of the earth are Chinese, and their country at the present time is more primitive, in the scarcity of railways, telegraphs, public utilities, and every provision conducing to comfort and common-sense living, than any other land pretending to civilization. It is a fact that outside of Shanghai, Canton, Pekin and Tientsin, the people do not want many of the products of the outer world; but it is a truism that much profit accrues from teaching Asiatics to "want" modern products.

The German Emperor foresaw that China could not much longer resist the invasion of outside enterprise and trade; and to his mind there could have been no suspicion of doubt that the victor in the awful contest could and would dictate trade terms and privileges everywhere in the Celestial Empire. If Japan won, the Japanese would surely exploit commercially their great neighbor, whose written language is nearly identical with their own—this would be but natural to the Mikado's people, teeming with aptitude as manufacturers and traders, and recognizing the necessity for recouping outlay in the war.

If Russia were successful, her reward would be the validating of her hold upon Manchuria, the bundling of the Japs out of Korea, and the attainment to a position of controlling influence in China's political affairs. The supplying of articles of general manufacture and commerce to the 400,000,000 people of China could have been no part of Russia's aspiration, for the reason that Russia is not a manufacturing country and has but little to sell. Her enormous tea bill to China is paid yearly in money, even. A nation seeking in time to control the whole of Asia could n't bother with commercial matters, certainly not. Yet, one of the fruits of victory in the war would have been the splendid opportunity to exploit trade everywhere in China—a privilege of priceless value.

What country was to benefit through this, with Russia's moral support and permission, had the Czar's legions been successful?

France? Hardly; for the French were bound by hard and fast alliance, and it had never been the policy at St. Petersburg to give anything material to France. Uncle Sam, whose people had financed half the war loans of Japan, could scarcely hope to extend his business in China with Russia's co-operation; nor could Japan's ally and moral supporter, John Bull.

Who, then, could stand in a likelier position to become legatee of this valued privilege than the Trade-Lord of Germany? The Emperor William had been Russia's "best friend" from the inception of the war, and was admittedly an adept in promoting trade, for his people had attained in a few years to an envied position in the commerce of the world. A quarter of the trade of "awakened" China would make Germany a vast workshop, a hive of industry. And this was precisely what the astute Hohenzollern saw through the smoke of battle in far-away Manchuria. He saw a prosperous Germany if the Slav crushed the yellow man. To say he did not would be a libel upon a giant intellect.

Any one disposed to review practically certain incidents in the recent history of Germany may develop a dozen reasons why the Emperor should seek to make his country all important through trade conquest. Let it be remembered that the Kaiser chafes at barriers of every kind, and that there is a boundlessness in his nature at times trying to his patience. He looks at the map of the German Empire and painfully admits that the present frontiers and area are practically those bequeathed by the great William. To a divine-right monarch this is exasperating. The loftiest ambition of a sovereign is to have the national area expand under his rule.

William's medieval temperament shudders at the crowded condition of the earth in this twentieth century, when all frontiers appear immovable. Had he lived in the days of the Crusaders his valiant sword would probably have brought all Palestine under German control; and had he been a free agent when Bonapartism collapsed he most likely would have carried the German standard to the Mediterranean, perhaps to Stamboul. The ironical fact is that the German Emperor has had rebuffs and disappointments in his efforts to expand his realm. The Monroe Doctrine, excluding his empire from even a coaling station in this hemisphere, is to the Kaiser a perpetual nightmare. Sturdy sons of the Fatherland control the trade of more than one republic in South and Central America, but nowhere is it possible to unfurl the standard of Germany over "colony" or "sphere of influence." To forcibly back up his subjects' pecuniary rights in the American hemisphere, even, the approval of the government at Washington has first to be obtained. In his heart the Kaiser loathes the doctrine of Monroe; that is obvious.

It is twenty years since Germany began to build up a colonial empire in Africa, and the net result is that, after spending some hundred million dollars, she has acquired over a hundred million square miles of territory, with a sparsely scattered German population of between five and six thousand souls. A third of the adult white population is represented by officials and soldiers. Militarism is rampant everywhere, with the result that the white settler shuns German colonies as he would the plague. The keen-witted Kaiser long ago saw that empire-building in the Dark Continent could produce nothing but expense during his lifetime.

"To perdition with the Monroe Doctrine, and with African tribes blind to the excellence of Ger-

EXHIBITION OF BODIES OF CHINESE MALEFACTORS WHO HAVE BEEN STRANGLED

man-made wares," the Kaiser might have said ten years ago: "I 'll have sweet revenge upon all and sundry by capturing trade everywhere—I 'll make Germany the workshop of the universe. Keep your territory, if you like; I 'll get the trade! Bah, Monroe Doctrine! Bah, grinning Senegambians!"

The resolute Trade-Lord then turned his face to the bountiful Orient, pregnant with resource beyond the dreams of avarice, teeming with hundreds of millions of people. The East had made England dominant in the world's affairs. Keeping his soldiers at home, the Kaiser hurled a legion of trade-getters into the Far East, planting commercial outposts in Ceylon, sending a flying column of bagmen and negotiators to India and the Straits Settlements, and distributing a numerical division of business agents throughout China. The Empire of the Celestials was made the focal point of a great propaganda, openly espoused by the Emperor.

It was readily demonstrated that Great Britain had no permanent control of commerce in the East, not even in her own possessions. The Teuton, for a time content with trifling profit, underbid all rivals—and orders and contracts poured into Germany. Belgian products competed only in price; and American manufacturers seemed too busy in providing goods for home use to seriously try for business in Asia—they booked orders coming practically unsought, that was about all. The Chino-Japanese conflict of a dozen years ago, although disastrous to China's army, stimulated the absorbing power of the Chinese for goods of western manufacture, and Germany sold her wares right and left.

Important steamship lines were then subsidized by the German government to maintain regular services between Germany and the Far East, carrying goods and passengers at reasonable charges: and it was known that in his personal capacity the Emperor had become a large shareholder in one of them. Germany was prospering, and the Trade-Lord and his lieutenants were happy. All recognized the possibilities of Oriental business. China was preparing to throw off the conservatism and lethargy of centuries, and trade was the key-note of everything pertaining to Germany's relations with the Pekin government. German diplomatists on service in China were instructed to employ every good office to induce German business, and the Kaiser himself selected and instructed consular officials going to the Flowery Kingdom. Able commercial attachés, with capacity for describing trade conditions, were maintained there, and required to be as industrious as beavers. For trade-promoting capacity German consuls in China have no equal—and they all know that the Kaiser's interest in Chinese trade amounts to mania.

The assassination in the streets of Pekin, in 1900, of Minister von Kettler, Germany's envoy, and the subsequent sending of an imperial prince of China to Berlin to express the regrets of the

Chinese government, strengthened materially the Kaiser's hold upon Chinese affairs. Reiteration from Washington of the "open door" in China struck no terror to the Kaiser, justified in believing he could hold his position against all comers. As proof of this belief he might point to German steamers in Hong Kong and Shanghai literally vomiting forth each week thousands of tons of goods "Made in Germany," penetrating every section of China even to the upper waters of the Yang-tse. A few years ago nearly all this trade was exclusively British.

The question of Chinese exclusion and the threatened boycott of American goods by China was the occasion of anxiety in this country—but none in Germany. It is well appreciated that the spread of the sentiment in the East that the United States is unjust to Chinamen of the better class might undo the splendid work of Secretary Hay in cultivating the friendship of the Celestial Empire by standing fast for China's administrative entity and insisting on the "open door" policy.

Knowing that the "awakening" of China would be one of the results of the war, the Master Mind in Berlin had not long to consider where the interest of Germany lay, for he well knew that if they conquered, the Japs might in a few years supply the kindred Chinese with practically every article needed from abroad.

If Russia won, then "Best Friend" William of Germany, one of the most irresistible forces in the world, would have a freer hand in China than ever—and this would mean a prosperous Germany for years to come.

By directing the sympathies of the German people to the Russian side, the Kaiser played a trump card in statecraft, certainly. As a soldier, William II must have known the fighting ability and prowess of the little men of Japan, for German officers had for years been the instructors of the Mikado's army—but the public attitude of the head of a government must ever be that which best serves the State. Whatever the chagrin at Berlin over Russia's defeat, a battle royal will be needed for Japan to overcome Germany's lead in Chinese trade; but in time Japan will have this, provided she is well advised and has the tact to play fair with Uncle Sam and his commercial rights.

What of the German colony in China—Kiau-chau, on the east coast of the Shan-tung peninsula, whose forts frown upon the Yellow Sea? Is there anything like it, strategically and trade wise, in the East? When the Kaiser's glance falls upon the map of Kiau-chau, and he recalls the ease with which he segregated from Pekin's rule a goodly piece of old China, he may be irreverently moved to the extent of again snapping his fingers at the Monroe Doctrine, and at millions of simple Africans who refuse to eat German foods and wear not a stitch of German fabrics. Kiau-chau represents the cleverest feat of colony-building the world has seen since the great powers declared a closure to land-grabbing in the East.

SIMPLE PUNISHMENT OF A CHINESE MENDICANT

The Kaiser's Play for Chinese Trade

When some German missionaries were murdered a few years since in China, the Kaiser, ever an opportunist, was justly angry, and Pekin shuddered at the possibility of national castigation. "Could the Mighty One at Berlin condone the offense if China gave Germany a harbor to be used as coaling station and naval headquarters?" "Possibly; but how can China bestow territory, in view of the American government's certainty to insist that there be no parceling of China, none whatever?"

"Easily managed," was the reply. "It need not be a transfer of territory, but a 'lease,' say for ninety-nine years. This would save China's 'face,' and not disturb the powers."

Hence a "lease" was prepared for all the territory bounded in a semi-circle drawn fifteen miles from Kiau-chau bay—a goodly piece in all conscience. Then came *pourparlers* for greater German authority, and more territory. As a consequence, in a supplementary document signed at Pekin, it was additionally agreed that "in a further zone thirty miles from all points of the leased territory the Chinese government shall no longer for a space of ninety-nine years be entitled to take any step without previous authorization from the German government."

This amounted in substance to saying farewell on China's part to a slice of domain in all more than twice the size of the state of Rhode Island. The "sphere of influence," so-called, measures 2,750 square miles. Germany was given as well the equivalent of sovereignty over the harbor of Kiau-chau, no end of mining and railway rights, and other privileges. The lease dates from March 6th, 1898. England was to give Wei-hai-wei back to China should Russia retire or be driven from Port Arthur, but has not done so. In all probability Germany, as well as Great Britain, is located on the Yellow Sea under a tenure that will be found to be permanent.

Kiau-chau harbor is one of the most spacious and best protected on the coast of China. The small native town of Tsing-tau, admirably situated on the harbor, was adopted by Germany as the seat of government, and all the appurtenances of a military and naval station have there been erected. A look of permanency characterizes every structure. The house of the naval governor is even pretentious. The capital is laid out with generous regard to broad streets, designated on name-plates as "strasses." A bank and hotels await the coming of business. The harbor has been dredged, and two miles of the best wharves in Asia constructed of masonry. Warehouses, barracks, hospitals, administrative buildings and coal sheds are there, all in German style, and intended to last hundreds of years.

Tsing-tau as a seat of deputed government may not have found its way into school-books—but the inquisitive traveler in Northeast China readily learns of its existence. Perhaps it is meant to be complimentary to China to retain the name Tsing-tau—but that is all about the place that is Chinese, save the coolies executing the white man's behest. There are 3,000 Europeans, almost exclusively Germans, in William II's capital on Kiau-chau Bay. Soldiers and officials predominate, of course, but merchant and industrial experts are in the pioneer band in conspicuous number.

And what of the "hinterland," compassed by the 45-mile semicircle, dotted with thirty odd native towns, the whole having a population of 1,200,000? This patch of China is surely in process of being awakened: there are numerous schools wherein European missionaries are teaching the German language, and enterprise greets the eye everywhere. Locomotives "Made in Germany" screech warnings to Chinese yokels to clear the way for trains heavy with merchandise of German origin—and this is but an incident in the great scheme of Germanizing the Chinese Empire. Incidentally, it is provided by the agreement between the Pekin and Berlin governments that a native land-owner in the leased section can sell only to the German authorities. This ruling conveys a meaning perfectly clear.

Less than a hundred miles up-country are the enormous coal fields of Weihsien and Poshan, by agreement worked with German capital, and connected with the harbor by railways built with German money and so devoted to Teutonic interests that the name of the company is spread on the cars in the language of the dear old Fatherland. The whole is a magnificent piece of propagandism, surely.

And what is back of it? What is the purpose of the appropriation of 14,000,000 marks for Kiau-chau in last year's official budget of the German government? Trade, little else; and Trade spelled best with a large T. Kiau-chau is a free port, like Hamburg. Why not make it the Hamburg of the East? is the question asked wherever German merchants foregather and affairs of the nation are discussed. From the standpoint of German trade, an Eastern Hamburg is alluring and laudatory—but few American manufactures, let it be plainly stated, will penetrate China through a gateway so controlled.

America's seeming indifference to Chinese trade, let it plainly be stated, is the only solace that commercial Europe is finding in our wonderful national growth. The subject is almost never referred to in the columns of British journals, nor in those of Germany, France, or Belgium. But manufacturers and exporters of these countries need no spur from their newspapers—without the accompaniment of beating drums all are seeking to make the Chinese their permanent customers. And, buttressed by undeniable advantages, Japan takes up the quest and means to spread her goods, largely fabricated from Uncle Sam's raw products, wherever the tenant of the earth be a Mongol.

Could a human being be more complaisant, more materially philanthropic, than the United States manufacturer or other producer? He surely cannot be blind to the undebatable fact that America

CHINESE BUDDHIST PRIESTS

cannot always wax opulent on home trade alone; he must know that in time we are certain to reach a period of overproduction, when it will aid the nation to have alien peoples for customers of our mills and workshops. Every land in Asia east of Singapore can be commercially exploited by the United States more easily, and with greater success, than by any other people, if the task be gone about systematically and practically.

The Chinese envoy of a few years ago to Washington, Minister Wu, said many wise things, and no epigram fell from his lips containing a profounder sermon for the American people than when he remarked that two inches added to the length of the skirts of every Chinese would double the market value of every pound of cotton.

Small as it was, our commerce in China was severely lessened last year, not alone by the boycott, but through the enterprise shown by other nations having a share in Celestial trade. The cotton cloth exports of the United States to China and Manchuria for the nine months ending September 30 fell off by over ten million dollars as compared with the same period of 1905. The respective amounts were $15,416,152 and $25,566,286. The Chinese buyers gave preference to the British, taking $34,245,129 worth of cotton fabrics from the United Kingdom for the first nine months of 1906, a decrease of $3,770,584 from last year. The British loss on bleached and gray goods was about half that of America's total loss, but the English exporters made up a large part of the shortage by much larger sales of printed and dyed goods. But while America remained almost stationary last year in selling cotton manufactures to the world, Great Britain made a tremendous stride. Her cotton fabric exports for the first nine months of 1906 were valued at a little more than two hundred and seventy-six million dollars, an increase of about twenty million dollars over the same period of 1905, and of nearly fifty million dollars over the first nine months of 1904. This was accomplished almost wholly by marketing wares wrought from fiber grown in our Southern States, let it be remembered.

And what would happen to British trade, let us inquire, were America to cease exporting raw cotton, to permit our staple to emerge from our land in a manufactured state, only?

The mere suggestion of the thing is sufficient to cause a cold shudder to play down the spinal column of John Bull. But the American people will never play the game of commerce in that way.

CHAPTER XV

JAPAN'S COMMERCIAL FUTURE

A NATION has risen in the Far East that is earning high place among enlightened governments, and in all probability the new-comer may already be entitled to permanently rank with the first-class powers of the earth. Japan is day by day a growing surprise to the world

That the diminutive Island Empire should have been able to humble the Muscovite pride was no greater marvel than that she should in a brief half-century advance from the position of a weak and unknown country to the station of a highly civilized nation. The government of the Mikado is to-day the best exponent of Asiatic progressiveness. And of a people with a capacity to perform in two generations such amazing things who shall dare say what to them is impossible?

Europe has never been in joyful mood over the rise in Japanese prestige, and she was more than reluctant to recognize the New Japan as the dominant force in the East. That a yellow people should claim fellowship with European countries guided by houses of lofty lineage was never believed to be possible. Continental Europe was unprepared to admit that Japan's triumph proved anything beyond a genius in the art of war that was nothing short of a menace to the rest of mankind, and that luck and geographical position helped the Mikado's legions in all ways. The great Hohenzollern spoke of the Japanese as the "scourge of God"; in France the "yellow peril" —a phrase really made in Germany—was seriously debated; while Russia many times sought sympathy from the Christian world on the ground that she was fighting the white man's battle against paganism. Solitary in her preference for the Japanese, expressed in the form of an astute and fortunate alliance, England gloried when her Oriental ally revealed the weakness of the vaunted power of the north that had dared to cast covetous eyes at India. All these nations hold Asiatic possessions, each has aspired to have a say in Chinese affairs, and each confesses to having a panacea for the innumerable ills of the Celestial Empire—each is hungry, likewise, to extend her trade with the awakening Orient.

Japan intruded, and deranged the plans of all and sundry for rousing China to a realization of her greatness; and in all human probability Japan will do for herself what several European powers wanted to do for Asia. Japan can always justify her claim that she was driven to war to preserve her national existence, by pointing to her rapidly-increasing population, existing in an archipelago incapable of producing food for even two thirds of her people, since every possibility of obtaining a foothold on the adjacent continent had been cut off by self-imposed Russian rule. There was no room for expansion, that was clear.

When Japan shattered the strength of Russia she gained many coveted advantages. One of these was the opportunity to commercialize neighboring Korea, a goodly section of Manchuria, and practically the whole of China—enough to recoup the war's outlay; and once entered upon, why not perfect and extend the enterprise wherever she might, thereby providing occupation for her increasing millions of people?

For a long time to come Japan will remain conspicuously in the public eye, but her achievements and victories hereafter are to be those of peace. Her scheme for national betterment, already well under way, is as thoughtfully prepared as was her war program. The Mikado's people emerged from the Russian conflict with energies enormously aroused, and a few months later every condition was favorable to a realization of the dream of empire giving to Japan an importance amounting almost to sovereignty over a vast section of the Far East. The new treaty with Great Britain, which Germans claimed to be anything but altruistic, is having a steadying influence on the policy of the Tokyo government.

With the conversion of Japan from war to peace, the process of fiscal recuperation and industrial development has been observed by students of Eastern affairs with the keenest interest. The debt of the nation at the close of the war in 1905 was approximately $870,000,000, which sum, apportioned among Nippon's 47,000,000 inhabitants, was $18.71 per capita. The amount properly chargeable to the campaign was $600,000,000, or thereabouts. A characteristic of the war commanding widespread attention was that the Japanese side was conducted from start to finish on the soundest financial principles, with her credit abroad scarcely lessened by successive bond issues. It was the criticism of students of finance that Japan conducted her campaign throughout on a gold basis, as if exploiting a vast commercial program, without subjecting herself to usurious commissions, and without resorting to the issuance of fiat or negligible currency. The financing of the Asiatic side of the great Russo-Japanese conflict was certainly as businesslike as anything ever done by a European power compelled to raise funds by foreign bond sales.

When a candid history of the war is penned, the writer must perforce acknowledge the "luck" attaching to Japan when Russia expelled the Jews, and when thousands of that faith were ruthlessly slaughtered at Kishineff. Whether the purse-strings of the world are controlled by Hebrew bankers may be a moot question, but it was a fact distinctly clear that Japan could place her bonds in any money-lending country in the world, while Russia could scarcely raise a rouble upon her foreign credit. Even Germany, the sentimental ally of Russia, almost begged for the privilege of lending to Japan. There was no disputing that the great Hebraic banking houses of London, New

BRONZE DAIBUTSU AT KAMAKURA, JAPAN

York and Frankfort found it an easy task to supply the Mikado's country with every needed sinew of war, and the massacres of Kishineff may have been avenged in a measure at Port Arthur and Mukden.

The ambitious and sturdy people of Japan are indisposed to regard the war debt as an excessive burden, and it is their determination to treat their bonded obligations as a spur to active industry. It must be confessed that Japan's debt is but a trifle less than that of the United States, and is carried at double the interest rates of the American debt; and further, that Japan's total area is smaller than that of our state of California. The portentous aspect of the national obligation of Japan is that it must absorb in interest charges fully a third of the empire's income for many years of peace and prosperity to come.

A large part of the debt incurred before the war was for public works, most of which are productive. Funds realized from early loans, both foreign and domestic, as well as a portion of the income from the indemnity earned by the war with China, were invested in commercial enterprises owned or fostered by the empire, and the government receives a considerable benefit from the public railways, tobacco monopoly, woolen mills, and a few other industrial ventures. The railways are extremely profitable, and the large sums spent in the creation of post-offices, telephone and telegraph lines, port facilities, etc., have proved wise investments.

Observers of national statistics have long known

that a country without heavy indebtedness amounts to little in a worldly and industrial sense. Abundantly solvent, France has a debt averaging $151.70 per person, and the United Kingdom (Great Britain and Ireland), a pro rata debt of $91.80. Portugal owes $143.82 per subject, Holland $90.74, and Belgium $75.63. The heaviest governmental obligation is that of Australia, averaging $263.90 per inhabitant; and the lightest responsibility among important nations is that of the United States, gradually lessening, now standing at but $10.93. Our Cuban neighbors, owing $21.88 per capita, make little complaint of fiscal burden. Whether a debt be burdensome or otherwise depends as much upon the character of the people as upon natural resources. Decaying Portugal could not by industry liberate herself from pecuniary thraldom in a century, while the Japanese probably could liquidate every obligation in fifteen years, were they pressed to do so.

No country can present a better foundation for industrial and commercial development at this time than Japan, and the signing at Portsmouth of the peace agreement marked the beginning of an era of national growth that may challenge the admiration of the world as did the feats of arms of Oyama and Togo. The war cemented classes in Japan almost to a condition of homogeneity—practically every subject of the Mikado believed in the necessity for the conflict, and made sacrifices to contribute to the cost thereof. Distinctions of class are now seldom thought of, and it contributes mightily to the material improvement of a nation to have a single language. The descendants of the samurai class acknowledge now the need for trade on a grand scale, and they are only too ready to embark in manufacturing and trading enterprises. There are scarcely ten great fortunes in the realm, and the number of subjects removed from activity by even moderate affluence is remarkably small. Likewise, the number of persons reckoned in the non-producing class, through dissipation or infirmity, is insignificant. And, more potent than all these reasons uniting to assist in the expansion of Japanese industry and thrift, is the intense patriotism of the people, stimulated by glorious success in two wars against foreign nations of overwhelming populations, as well as the recognition from high and low that Japan's golden opportunity has arrived. Almost to a man the Japanese want to employ their sinews and intellect in elevating the Land of the Rising Sun to an honored place among progressive nations.

The Japanese exchequer is at present a long way from depletion, by reason of the $150,000,000 loan secured in America, England and Germany. Probably two thirds of this remained unexpended. Many Tokyo bankers believed the loan unnecessary, inasmuch as there were funds in hand sufficient to finance the war well into 1906, had peace not been agreed upon. But the flotation was deemed wise, not alone because of prevailing ease in the money market, but for the effect that an oversubscribed loan in America and Europe would have upon the Czar's government. The portion of the loan remaining unused for war was employed for giving effect to Japan's industrial propaganda, and presumably has been spent for the endless machinery demanded by the factories and shipyards that are transforming Japan into a vast workshop, for structural metal, and for steel rails, cars and locomotives for railways in Manchuria and Korea; and generally for the hundred and one purposes playing a part in the development of lands hitherto out of step in the march of enterprise, and where strife has until recently stifled the usual manifestations of man's desire to improve his surroundings. The Japanese government in 1906 purchased six railways, which were profit earners, paying for them $125,000,000 in five per cent. bonds that may be redeemed in five years.

There is no likelihood of a reduction in Japan's debt for a long time, but its weight upon the people may be reduced by conversions. As the national credit strengthens, the interest on borrowings may be correspondingly decreased. Consequently, there may be frequent funding operations and new issues, until seven and six per cent. bonds have given place to obligations bearing five per cent. interest or less. To provide funds for early railway building, considerable capital was borrowed at as high a rate as ten per cent. When these obligations expire all necessary money can be found in the country at less than half the original rate. Japan is fortunate in having many sound financiers to invite to her official councils, and it is helpful to the country that Tokyo and Yokohama bankers are competent and progressive. These men pronounce Japan's present financial position sound, and claim that the country can easily carry the existing debt.

In natural resources Japan is not well to do, it must be frankly said. Examine the country in as friendly a spirit as one may, little is developed to support any statement that the country may become prosperous from the products of her own soil. In truth Japan is nearly as unproductive as Greece and Norway, for only sixteen per cent. of her soil is arable. The mountain ranges and peaks and terraced hills that make the country scenically attractive to the tourist come near to prohibiting agriculture. The lowlands, separating seacoast from the foothills, and the valleys generally, are given over to rice culture, and these contribute largely towards sustaining the people. Where valleys are narrow, and on hillside patches, cultivation is carried on wholly by hand. In recent years phosphates and artificial fertilizers have been encouraged by the government, and with the educational work now in hand science may give an increase of crops from the circumscribed tillable area. The country's forests cannot be sacrificed, and grazing lands for flocks and herds scarcely exist.

A recent magazine writer, holding a doleful view of Japan's agricultural condition, wholly overlooked the silk and tea crops in his search for native products, an error obviously fallen into through the fact that these are not raised on what governmental reports call "tillable ground,"—meaning that they are produced outside the sixteen per cent. arable area. Silk is Japan's important salable crop, two thirds of which is exported in its raw state. In the past few years the silk exports have averaged $55,000,000. Japan grows the tea consumed in the country, and sends annually $6,500,000 worth to market.

If the rice crop might be exported it would realize $200,000,000 each year. But no food may be sent abroad, for it is a sad fact that Japan is capable of feeding only two thirds of her own people. It is necessary to import foodstuffs to the extent of about $47,000,000 a year. The Japanese benefit by the compensating supply of fish secured from the seas washing the shores of the Island Empire. When it is realized that Japan's rapidly-growing population cannot be sustained by her soil and fisheries, the real reason for battling against Russia's aggression on the mainland is understood, for ten years hence, Japan's crowding millions, confined to her own islands, would experience the pangs of hunger. The Mikado and his councilors foresaw this.

"Having deposits of coal and iron, why may not Japan be developed into the Eastern equivalent of England?" ask stay-at-home admirers of the Japanese, who believe that to them nothing is impossible. The Mikado's territory has coal, iron and copper, it is true; but in no instance is the mineral present to an extent making it a national as-

A GARDEN VIEW OF THE AMERICAN EMBASSY, TOKYO

set of importance. Bituminous coal of good quality is mined at several points which is used by Japanese commercial and naval vessels; but elsewhere in the East it has to compete with Chinese and Indian coals. It is said in Nagasaki that her coal will last another two centuries, but were it mined on the scale of American and British coal it would be exhausted in a generation. The greatest efforts have been made to produce iron ore in paying quantities. In several instances public assistance has been lent to the industry, but seldom has a ton of ore been raised that has not cost twice its market value. Japan is determined to become a producer of iron, and to this end a long lease had been secured on an important mineral tract in China, whose ore blends advantageously with Mexican and Californian hematite, while it is asserted that the government has secured in Manchuria a seam of coal fifty feet in thickness, covered by a few feet of soil, that is contiguous to transportation, and which cannot be exhausted in hundreds of years. A valuable acquisition in conquered Saghalien—not noted by the newspapers—is beds of coal and iron of vast area. These may enable Japan, in her determination to become a manufacturing nation, to be eventually independent of other countries for basic supplies. But success in this direction is problematical, to say the least.

For two thousand years Japan has mined copper in a limited way, but the production of the metal is carried on at present without much profit. When the Chinese government requires a vast quantity of copper the order is sent to the United States. Japan cannot be considered as a producer of minerals of sufficient importance to aspire to a profitable career through them, for the yearly aggregate value of all minerals, including gold from the Formosa mines, is not more than $20,000,000.

The inevitable query in the reader's mind is, How is the Jap, knowing it is now or never with him—and cognizant that he is poor in all save ambition and enterprise—going to create for his beloved Nippon a position of prominence and security in the fast-rushing, selfish world? Every intelligent Japanese is aware of the slenderness of his country's resources, and yet every son of the Chrysanthemum Realm throbs with desire to see Japan a first-class and self-supporting power, honored and respected throughout the universe.

The Japanese possess some quality of golden value, otherwise cautious capitalists in America and Europe would never have lent them $360,000,000. What is it?

Japan's asset of importance is the awakened energy of her people—this was the soundest security back of the bond issues. It won the war over Russia, and persons familiar with the Japanese character believe it is now going to win commercially and industrially. Better proof of this is not wanted than the fact that Japanese bonds stood as firm as the rock of Gibraltar on the world's exchanges when it became known that Russia was to pay no indemnity. The information provoked street riots in Tokyo, but Japanese securities moved only fractionally in New York and London.

Two countries have long been keenly observed by enlightened Japanese. They study America as a model industrial land, and get manufacturing ideas from us; but they look to Great Britain for everything having to do with empire, with aggrandizement, and with diplomacy. To them England is a glittering object lesson of a nation existing in overcrowded islands extending its rule to other lands and other continents, producing endless articles needed by mankind, and carrying these to the ends of the earth in their own ships. These Japanese have perceived that the interchange of commodities between most countries of the globe is preponderatingly in the hands of the British—in fact, that the enterprise of British merchant or British ship-owner has placed practically the universe under tribute.

May not insular Japan become in time the Asiatic equivalent of Great Britain? Japan is advantageously located, and by common consent is now dominant in the Far East. Years ago England ceased to be an agricultural country, and the products of British workshops now buy food from other nations and allow for the keeping of a money balance at home. Nature has decreed that Japan can never be an agricultural land. Why, then, may she not do what England has done? England has her India, pregnant with the earth's bounty, and her Australia, yet awaiting completer development by man. Why may not the great Middle

Kingdom become the handmaiden of Japan, without disturbing dynastic affairs, and primitive Korea be a fair equivalent of the Antipodean continent? It is known to be Japan's plan to permanently colonize Korea and Manchuria, teeming in agricultural and mineral riches, with her surplus population.

"Prestige and opportunity make this attainable," insist the ambitious sons of Japan; "and while it is probably too late to expand the political boundaries of our empire, we surely may make Nippon the seat of a mighty commercial control, including in its sphere all of China proper, Manchuria and Korea—welding them into 'commercial colonies' of Japan." This is precisely what the modern Japanese wants his country to do, and this Japanization of the Far East is an alluring project, certainly.

"But are not these 'open-door' countries, stipulated and guaranteed by the powers—meaning that your people can enjoy no special trade advantage in them?" the American asks the man of Japan.

"Emphatically are they open to the trade and enterprise of all comers: but there are four potential advantages that accrue to the benefit of the Japanese at this time—geographical position, necessity for recouping the cost of the war, an identical written language, and superabundance of capable and inexpensive labor. With these advantages and practical kinship we fear no rivalry in the creation of business among the Mongol races," adds the man speaking for the New Japan.

It calls for little prescience to picture a mighty Japanese tonnage on the seas in the near future. Next to industrial development, the controlling article of faith of the awakened Japan is the creation of an ocean commerce great enough to make the Japanese the carriers of the Orient. There can be nothing visionary in this, for bountiful Asia is almost without facilities for conveying her products to the world's markets. Indeed, were present-day Japan eliminated from consideration, it would be precise to say that Asia possessed no oversea transportation facilities.

The merchant steamship is intended to play an important rôle in Japan's elevation. Shipping is to be fostered by the nation until it becomes a great industry, and it is the aim of the Mikado's government to provide for constructing ships for the public defence up to 20,000 tons burden, and making the country independent of foreign yards through being able to produce advantageously commercial vessels for any requirement. Japan is blind neither to the costliness of American-built ships nor to the remoteness of European yards. The war with Russia was not half over when it was apparent that Japan would not longer be dependent upon the outer world for vessels of war or of commerce. In the closing weeks of 1906 there was completed and launched in Japan the biggest battleship in the world, the *Satsuma,* constructed exclusively by native labor. She is of about the dimensions of the *Dreadnaught,* of the British navy, but claimed to be her superior as a fighting force. The launching of the *Satsuma,* witnessed by the Emperor, was regarded as a great national event.

In the war with China, twelve or thirteen years ago, Japan had insufficient vessels to transport her troops. The astute statesmen at Tokyo, recognizing the error of basing the transportation requirements of an insular nation upon ships controlled by foreigners, speedily drafted laws looking to the creation of a native marine which might be claimed in war time for governmental purposes. The bestowal of liberal bounties transformed Japan in a few short years from owning craft of the junk class to a proprietorship of modern iron-built vessels of both home construction and foreign purchase. In the late campaign there was no comparison in the seamanship of the agile son of Nippon and that of the hulking peasant of interior Russia. The Jap was proven time and again to be the equal of any mariner. Native adaptability and willingness to conform to strict discipline, unite in making the Japanese a seaman whose qualities will be telling in times of peace.

Of late years hundreds of clever young Japanese have served apprenticeships in important shipyards in America, England, Germany and France, with the result that there are to-day scores of naval architects and constructors in Japan the equals of any in the world. Whether as designers, yard managers or directors of construction, the Japs, with their special schooling, have nothing to learn now from foreign countries. The genius of some of these men played a part in Togo's great victory.

Japanese men of affairs pretend to see little difficulty in the way of their nation controlling the building of ships for use throughout the East. Local yards are already constructing river gunboats and torpedo craft for the Chinese government, and it is reasonable to believe that a year or two hence their hold upon the business will amount practically to a monopoly. British firms with yards at Singapore, Hong Kong and Shanghai are not rejoiced at the prospect of Japanese rivalry. It is possible that the Japanese may become shipbuilders for our own Philippine archipelago.

Already the shipyards of Nippon are ringing with the sound of Japan's upbuilding; and the plant of the Mitsubishi company, at Nagasaki—among the largest in the world,—has been enlarged to accommodate increasing demands. The enormous *Minnesota,* of the Great Northern Steamship Company, was not so long ago repaired at Nagasaki in a dry-dock having eighty feet in length to spare.

Japanese steamship lines already extend to Europe, Australia, Bombay, Eastern Siberia, China, Korea and Saghalien, and to San Francisco and Puget Sound ports. A company has been formed to develop a service between Panama, the Philippines and Japanese ports, in anticipation of the completion of the Panama Canal: and, further perceiving the opportunity rapping at her door, Japan is preparing to place a line on the ocean that will bring the wool, hides and grain of the River Plate region to Japanese markets at the minimum of expense. The undisguised purpose of this South-American venture is to get cheap wheat from Argentina. Rice eating in Japan is giving way to bread made from wheat, or from a mixture of wheat and rice and other cereals. It is further known that Japan is casting covetous eyes on the trade of Brazil, and the line to the Plate may be extended to Brazilian ports.

In 1894 Japan had only 657,269 tons of merchant shipping; she has now upwards of a million tons, represented by 5,200 registered vessels. Almost half the steamers entering Japanese ports fly the flag of the Rising Sun, and Japan's tonnage at this time is greater than that of Russia, Austria, Sweden, Spain, Denmark or Holland. In the matter of oversea tonnage, Japan is far ahead of the United States. One fleet of Japanese mail steamers, the Nippon Yusen Kaisha, whose president, Rempei Kondo, is one of Japan's most progressive men, is numerically and in tonnage larger than any ocean line under the Stars and Stripes. It has seventy ships, aggregating 236,000 tons. A dozen of its vessels, making the service between Yokohama and London, are fourteen-knot ships.

These facts should be considered by every American complacently believing that the traffic of the countries and islands washed by the Pacific is open to American enterprise whenever we bid for it. When Eastern trade develops in magni-

JAPANESE JUNK, OR CARGO BOAT

tude, it may be found that the Japanese have laid permanent hold upon its carriage and interchange. John Bull, be it remembered, drove the American merchantman from the Atlantic; and likewise Japan may capture the carrying business of the Pacific. It must be obvious that the nation controlling the transportation of the Far East will seek to control its trade: and it is sounding no false alarm to cite facts and conditions showing that the awakening lands of Eastern Asia have more in store for energetic Japan than for the United States, now fattening inordinately on home trade—when overproduction comes, as it surely will, it then may be found difficult to supplant another people in the occupation of conveying American commodities to Eastern markets. There are persons in the Orient, none too friendly to America, who expect to see the commercial flag of Japan paramount on the Pacific eight or ten years hence.

If it be conceded that Japan will absorb the bulk of the shipping of the Pacific as it develops, valid reasons for fearing Japan as the trade competitor of the United States do not exist. Unquestionably Japan is to exploit the industry of her people; but the same poverty of resources making this imperative insures for Uncle Sam a valuable partnership in the program. Japan is bristling with workshops and mills in which a hundred forms of handiwork will be developed—and in a majority of these the adaptive labor of the empire will fabricate, from materials drawn from America, scores of forms of merchandise, which the Japanese propaganda will distribute throughout China, Manchuria, Korea and Japan—the "Great Japan," British publicists are calling it. Methods, materials, machinery, tools—all will be American.

Having made no systematic appeal for the trade of the Far East in its broadest sense, America enjoys but small share of it. In the past few years our exports to Japan, however, have grown rapidly—chiefly in raw cotton and other unmanufactured materials. With Japanese selling agents canvassing lands inhabited by a half billion people, the products of America are to have enhanced consumption. This trade in Mongol countries, although vicarious, may run to large dimensions.

The leading item of Japan's industrial promotion program is to become manufacturer of a goodly portion of the textiles worn in her vast "sphere of commerce." The Japanese have seen that the British Isles, growing not a pound of cotton, spin and weave the staple for half the people of the earth, and wish to profit by the example of their prosperous ally. To this end, cotton mills have sprung into being throughout Japan, in which American-grown fiber is transformed by the cheapest competent labor in the world into fabrics sold to China's and Japan's millions. It is certain that the controlling manufacture of Japan will be cotton, and the production of woolen cloths may come next. It is interesting to know that Japan increased the value of her exports of cotton manufactures to China from $251,363 in 1894 to $16,126,054 in 1904.

"Why not fabricate her own raw silk, and send it to market ready for wear?" asks the foreigner reluctant to believe that Japan can hope to compete with Lancashire in the spinning of cotton. The answer is simple—it is because America is the principal purchaser of the raw article. Were it brought across the Pacific in manufactured form, the duty on it would be almost prohibitive; in its unwrought state it enters the country free.

Great progress must be made before Japanese business may be considered a "menace" to any nation enjoying Eastern trade, for the yearly value of Japan's manufactures is now only about $150,000,000, an average of about $3 per capita of the population. America has single cities that produce more. The combined capital of all organized industrial, mining, shipping, banking and agricultural undertakings in Japan is $475,000,000, or less than half the capital of the United States Steel Corporation. The Mikado's empire is bound to Great Britain by a political alliance of unusual force, but industrial Japan must of necessity be linked to the United States by commercial ties even stronger. Distance between Europe and Japan, and excessive Suez Canal tolls, give unassailable advantage to the United States as purveyor of unwrought materials to the budding New England of the Far East.

The custom of speaking of our friends of the Island Empire as "the little Japanese," is a fault that should be promptly mended. Japan is small, it is true, but the people are numerous to the point of wonderment. Consequently, it can do no harm to memorize these facts: That Japan has an area actually 27,000 square miles greater than the British Isles, and 5,000,000 more inhabitants; in other words, the population of Japan is 47,000,000, while that of Great Britain and Ireland is but 42,000,000. That Japan's population exceeds that of France by 8,000,000, of Italy by 14,000,000, and of Austro-Hungary by nearly 2,000,000. That outside of Asia there are but three countries in all the world with greater populations than Japan—Russia, the United States, and Germany. There was reason for calling the Jap the "Yankee of the East," or the "Englishman of the Orient," for otherwise the phrases could not have been forced into popular use.

It is the judgment of many who have studied the Japanese at close range that they are endowed with attributes of mind and body which make them equal, man for man, with the people of America and Great Britain. Asiatic though they are, it will be unwise to permit the brain to become clogged with the idea that they are "Asiatics" in the popular acceptance of the word. The Japan of the present is the antithesis of "Asiatic," and the Japan of the near future promises to be a country best measured by Western standards.

The Japanese are athirst for knowledge, and impatient for the time to arrive when the world will estimate them at their intellectual value, and forget to speak of them as the little "yellow" men of the East. This is manifested to a visitor many times every day. Their greatest craving is to know English, not merely well enough to carry on trade advantageously, but to read understandingly books that deal with the moderate sciences, and other works generally benefiting. Yokohama and Tokyo possess a score of establishments where practically every important volume of instruction, whether it be English or American, is reproduced in inexpensive form, and widely sold. For many years English has been taught in Japan's schools, but thousands of boys and men in cities and towns are each year acquiring the language by study in odd hours.

Examine the dog-eared pamphlet in the hands of the lad assisting in the shop where you are purchasing something, and you are almost certain to find it an elementary English book. Merchants know English well, as a rule; but with many of them the desire for knowledge is not satisfied with the acquisition of English—they desire to know other languages. In Yokohama I know a merchant of importance whose English is so good that one is drawn to inquire where he learned it. The answer will be that he studied odd hours at home and when not serving customers. And the visitor may further be informed by this man that he is also studying German and French. A teacher of German goes to his house at six o'clock each morning and for two hours drills him in the language. Then, in the evening, after a long day spent at business, a French teacher instructs him in the graceful language of France. And this merchant is but a type of thousands of Japanese who are daily garnering knowledge.

It is a pleasing incident for the visitor from America to read of a meeting in the Japanese capital of the local Yale Alumni Association—quite as pleasing as to see base-ball played in every vacant field convenient to a large town. Returning schoolboys have carried the game home to their companions, and in the voyage across the Pacific it has lost none of its fine points. For thirty years and longer the Japs have been learning English with the industry of beavers. And ambition has been responsible for this, the dogged determination to be somebody, and the patriotic wish to see Japan stand with the progressive nations of the earth. The power to keep such a people down does not exist. Preparation is a subject never absent from the thoughts of the Japanese. It was preparation that gave them victory after victory over the creatures of the Czar. Now they are fairly launched upon a brilliant career in trade and commerce. But Japan can merely fabricate our raw materials, thereby occupying a field in Asia that up to now Uncle Sam has made no determined effort to secure.

INDEX

INDEX

Index

Index